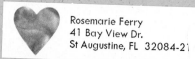

THE GOD OF HOPE AND THE END OF THE WORLD

*The God of Hope
and the
End of the World*

JOHN POLKINGHORNE

Yale University Press   *New Haven and London*

Published with assistance from the
Louis Stern Memorial Fund.

Scriptural quotations throughout this work are taken from
the New Revised Standard Version (NRSV).

Published 2002 in the United States by Yale University Press and in
Great Britain by SPCK Publishing.

Designed by James J. Johnson and set in Janson type by Tseng Information
Systems Inc., Durham, North Carolina.
Printed in the United States of America by R. R. Donnelley and Sons,
Harrisonburg, Virginia.

A catalogue record for this book is available from the Library of Congress
and the British Library.

ISBN: 0-300-09211-3 (cloth)
LOC Number: 2001046577

⊗ The paper in this book meets the guidelines for permanence and durability
of the Committee on Production Guidelines for Book Longevity of the
Council on Library Resources.

10 9 8 7 6 5 4 3 2 1

To
The Center of Theological Inquiry,
Princeton

and
my colleagues in the CTI Eschatology Project

Always be ready to make your defence to anyone who demands from you an account of the hope that is in you. (1 Peter 3:14)

Contents

II. Biblical Resources

III. Theological Approaches

CONTENTS

Acknowledgements

I am very grateful to the Center of Theological Inquiry, Princeton, and to its Director, Dr Wallace Alston, for generous hospitality both during deliberations of the CTI Eschatology Project (one of whose meetings was held in Heidelberg at the kind invitation of the Internationales Wissenschaftsforum) and also subsequently during a period of Membership of the Center that enabled me to complete the writing of this book. My intellectual debt to my colleagues on the Project will be obvious in the pages that follow. It is with sincere gratitude that I dedicate this book to these sources of stimulation and support.

I thank the staff of Yale University Press for their assistance in preparing the manuscript for press, and my wife, Ruth, for her help in correcting the proofs.

Introduction

For three years, an interdisciplinary group of scholars—scientists, social scientists, biblical scholars and theologians—met under the auspices of the Center of Theological Inquiry at Princeton. Their task was to reconsider, in the light of modern knowledge, the expression of Christian eschatological hope concerning the end of the world and concerning the fulfilment of the divine purpose for creation. One aspect of the group's activity was the evaluation of those currents of contemporary opinion about the shape and significance of the future that had been stirred up by the approach of the third Millennium. Another concern was how one may best articulate today the true nature of Christian hope and in what form one may credibly formulate and rationally defend the eschatological expectation of the attainment of God's goal for history. The results of our interaction were made available in a volume of essays entitled *The End of the World and the Ends of God*, edited by Michael Welker and myself.[1]

1. J. C. Polkinghorne and M. Welker (eds.), *The End of the World and the Ends of God*, Trinity Press International, 2000; referred throughout as *Ends*.

We believed that there is much of interest and value in that publication, but we also recognised that the essays there presented have varying degrees of specialisation and that they make significant intellectual demands on their readers. As its labours drew to a close, the group decided that there would also be merit in there being a smaller book, drawing inspiration from *Ends* but having the unity that would come from its having a single author. This second book would seek to address the issues in an intellectually serious manner, but it would be less full of scholarly detail than its parent volume. Since I like that kind of task, I volunteered to undertake this piece of writing and I was given the generous encouragement of my colleagues to set to work on the present volume.

This book is not a condensation or a digest of *Ends*. It will be clear, both explicitly in the quotations and references given and also implicitly in the lines of argument set down, that I am greatly indebted to the ideas and critiques that we shared together in the stimulating discussions of our group, and which were set out in our joint publication. Yet I have felt free to impose my own shaping on the material here presented and to state conclusions in accordance with my own beliefs and understanding. Inevitably, I have had to cover many topics on which I can make no claim to be an expert. This too has influenced the way in which this book has been written. For example, in the section relating to the biblical material, I have sought to survey themes derived from the Old and New Testaments generally, in contrast to the detailed scholarly exegeses of particular selected passages that are given in *Ends*.

Any treatment of eschatology requires the exploration of many kinds of insight, for it is concerned with what may be held to be a fitting fulfilment of the history of the universe and the history of humanity. Ultimately the issue is whether we live in a world that makes sense not just now, but totally and for ever. The thesis of this book is that Christian belief provides the essential resource for answering this fundamental question. That is the reason why the central section of my argument is concerned with a survey of biblical material and the final section develops theological reflection on the nature of eschatological hope. If, as I believe, any hope of a destiny beyond death can ultimately rest only on the faithfulness of God the Creator, then appeal to the revelatory insights by which that divine character has been made known is absolutely fundamental to the discussion. I understand revelation not as being propositional knowledge ineffably conveyed, but as the record of the particularly transparent people and events through which God has graciously shown forth the divine nature.[2] For the Christian, this awareness centres on the life, death and resurrection of Jesus Christ. Yet, while appeal to past experience and insight is indispensable, it is perfectly proper—indeed necessary—to ask how credible these eschatological assertions are today. Hence the discussion in the first section of material drawn from contemporary science and culture.

To a degree, the distinction between the three phases of the argument cannot be maintained and confined neatly within the three relevant sections of the book. The complex patterns interweaving together the three kinds of insight preclude an absolutely rigid separation, as will become clear as the argument is developed. Let me make it plain, also, that I

2. See J. C. Polkinghorne, *Faith, Science and Understanding*, SPCK/Yale University Press, 2001, ch. 3.

do not claim to 'prove' Christian eschatology. Proof is an inappropriately cut-and-dried category for the discussion of any kind of profound metaphysical issue. What I am seeking to do is to present the motivations for Christian eschatological hope and to show that this hope is one that is intelligible and defensible in the twenty-first century.

In the compass of a short book I have sought to paint a large canvas, with science, culture, scripture and theology all on the palette. Inevitably the brush strokes are bold, for I am seeking to convince by the significance of the whole, without essaying a meticulous depiction of every detail. One might say that the style is impressionistic rather than Flemish in its character. I hope that such a treatment will be found helpful and I direct the reader anxious for more minute discussion to consult the references given, including the essays in *Ends*.

The book begins with the exploration of the general setting within which contemporary eschatological thinking takes place. In chapter 1 we see that science presents us with the picture of a universe that, despite its present fruitfulness, will eventually end in the futility of cosmic collapse or decay. This reliable prediction poses a sharp question to theology concerning how the latter conceives of the ultimate fulfilment of God's creation. If the meta-story that theology seeks to tell is to carry conviction, it will have to include elements of both continuity and discontinuity in the linkages that it makes between the present universe and its destiny beyond its death.

Chapter 2 considers the features of current physical process that may be expected to be preserved as aspects of the continuity side of a credible eschatology. Of particular significance are both the way in which information is coming to take its place alongside energy in the fundamental conceptual vocabulary of twenty-first century science and also the role of temporal process in the unfolding history of the world. This chapter also surveys, and rejects as inadequate, certain metascientific responses that deny both the need and the possibility of looking beyond the extrapolation of present physical understanding.

Chapter 3 moves from the impersonal perspective of natural science to the more personal domain of the human sciences. The fundamental concept of hope is given some discussion in psychological terms, distinguishing it both from optimism and from wishful thinking. Brief notice is taken of claims relating to paranormal experiences, but the issues involved are considered to be too unclear and too uncertain to play any role in the subsequent development of the argument.

Chapter 4 moves on to consider some relevant issues arising from general culture. Stress is laid on the significance of a 'hot' cultural memory that engages with preceding generations in a way that liberates people from the limitation of the contemporary and releases them from a feeling of necessity to seek instant satisfaction. The shattered utopian dreams of the nineteenth century, and the demonic experiences of war and genocide in the twentieth century, have to be acknowledged and dealt with in the course of forming twenty-first century hopes and expectations. A generous metaphysical stance that transcends an arid physicalist reductionism, together with a 'thick' concept of the nature of temporality that delivers human beings from being in thrall to the immediate demands of the present, are both indispensable elements in framing an adequate context for eschatological thought.

Chapters 5 to 7 deal with the biblical material, surveying the scene in broad conceptual terms. Here we consider the foundational events and insights which, together with the continuing experience of the worshipping community of the Church, constitute the primary sources of Christian eschatological thinking. Central to the discussion in chapter 6 is the consideration of the evidence for the resurrection of Jesus Christ and the evaluation of the central role that his resurrection plays in Christian eschatological thinking. Paul's extended treatment of the relevant issues in 1 Corinthians 15 displays the apostle's engagement with the theme of continuity/discontinuity. Another important Pauline expression of the same eschatological tension is in terms of the old and new creations (chapter 7).

The final, theological section of the book reflects on the material that has gone before, seeking to make intelligible the hope of human and cosmic destinies beyond death and providing the warrant for such belief. It begins with a return to the theme of hope. Chapter 8 looks to the God whose steadfast love is the only ground of a true and everlasting hope. Sympathetic consideration is given to aspects of a realised eschatology located in the present (and particularly related to the eucharistic experience of the Church), but it is also claimed that a future-oriented element involving ultimate forgiveness and joy is indispensable to a fully articulated and convincing eschatology.

Chapter 9 considers how one may take the psychosomatic unity of humankind seriously and still retain a usable concept of the soul. The latter is conceived of as the information-bearing pattern carried by the matter of the body, a revival in modern dress of the Aristotelian-Thomistic idea of the soul as the form of the body. It is claimed to be a coherent hope that God will hold that pattern in the divine memory following its dissolution at death, and then finally restore a person's full humanity through the re-embodiment of the soul in the final great act of resurrection.

Chapter 10 considers what will be the context for that re-embodiment. It sees it as being the redeemed 'matter' of the new creation which will constitute the ultimate destiny of this present universe beyond its anticipated end in futility. The empty tomb has a key significance here as the enacted sign that matter as well as humanity participates in the seminal event of Christ's resurrection. This present world has the structure and physical fabric appropriate to a creation allowed to evolve and 'make itself' and it is, therefore, a universe in which death is the necessary cost of new life and a creation in which creatures exist at some epistemic distance from their Creator. However, it is perfectly coherent to believe that the new creation will be given a different character. It will be closely integrated with the energies and life of God and so its 'matter' may be expected to be endowed with different divinely bestowed properties that will free it from the shackles of transience and mortality. Nevertheless, it is also claimed that continuing, if redeemed, temporal process will be part of the new creation and some criticisms are made of the eschatological views of Wolfhart Pannenberg and Jürgen Moltmann that run contrary to this picture. Chapters 9 and 10 together set out the form of human hope as being death and resurrection, rather than some kind of spiritual survival.

Chapter 11 then considers the life of the world to come, organised around the theme of the Four Last Things: death, judgement, heaven, hell. Significant ideas that emerge include: the offer of divine mercy is not withdrawn at death, but neither will it be imposed on those who continue to refuse it post mortem; the hopefulness of eschatological expectation includes the understanding of a purgatorial process of judgement; the life of the world to come will have its own 'time' and history in which the redeemed participate in the unending exploration of the infinite riches of the divine nature.

In conclusion, chapter 12 points out certain differences between the approaches of systematic theologians and of scientist-theologians to eschatological matters. It then gives an account of John Hick's idea of eschatological verification and concludes by setting out four criteria whose satisfaction is necessary not only for an adequate eschatology, but also for a fully credible theology.

There are important elements in common between *Ends* and the present book. Both are based on a critical realist understanding of the nature of the scientific and theological enterprises.[3] Neither discipline is concerned merely with pragmatically useful manners of speaking but each seeks, within the necessary limitations of human ability to gain knowledge, to concern itself, respectively, with the world and with God as they actually are. In endeavouring to fulfil this task, both science and theology have to express their belief in the existence of unseen realities, be they confined quarks forever hidden within nuclear matter or be it the invisible reality of the divine presence. In each case, the justification for such a claim is the same: the appeal to what is not directly perceptible makes sense of great swathes of more accessible experience. It is the power to make experience intelligible that proffers us the key to the nature of reality. A realist understanding of the charac-

3. For a fuller discussion of these issues, see J. C. Polkinghorne, *Beyond Science*, Cambridge University Press, 1996, ch. 1; *Belief in God in an Age of Science*, Yale University Press, 1998, chs. 2 and 5.

ter of both science and theology is essential for the project of this book.

If science were not giving us verisimilitudinous knowledge of the nature of the physical world, its prognostications about the future of the universe would lose their force and the sharpness of the challenge they present to theology would be blunted. If theology were not concerned with a verisimilitudinous understanding of the nature of a faithful Creator, its attempts to speak of eschatological matters would amount to no more than the disguised exercise of a technique of consolation for the uncertainties of the present. It is because both, in their different ways, are telling us about the reality within which we live, that they are capable of fruitful interaction with each other.

This interaction is of particular significance for eschatology. The ground bass of the discussion, both here and in *Ends*, is the necessity of an interplay between continuity and discontinuity in speaking of God's purposes beyond the end of history. Without an element of continuity, the story of the eschaton would simply be a second story, with no coherent connection with the presently unfolding story of this creation. Those of us who are participants in the present process of the world would have no role or interest in that second story. Without an element of discontinuity, however, that second story would simply be a redundant repetition of the first. This duality of sameness and change is implied in the Christian tradition by the use of phrases such as 'the new creation' and 'the resurrection of the body'. It will be a principal preoccupation in what follows to explore what meaning can, with integrity, be attached today to such a combination of continuity and discontinuity. Science has a role to play in this discussion because its account of present process can offer insight into what aspects of that process's character may be expected to be preserved in fulfilling the constraint of continuity. For its part, theology can offer insight into how God's free action may be expected to bring about the kind of discontinuity essential for the ultimate fulfilment of the divine purpose. For the Christian theologian, a prime source of this latter insight will be the resurrection of Jesus Christ. It is the element of discontinuity—the expectation of the unexpected—that distinguishes theological eschatology from a secular futurology.[4]

My conviction is that it is a rich theological account, Trinitarian and incarnational in its foundations, that alone will furnish the basis of a defensible and intelligible eschatological hope in the twenty-first century. A scientist-theologian colleague, Arthur Peacocke, has recently expressed a different view:

> Furthermore, we have to ask, in what is much Christian eschatological talk of eschatology and the future based? Cosmology predicts with very great certainty the demise of this planet and all life on it, including ours. What is the cash value of talk about "a new heaven and a new earth"? The only propounded basis for this seems to me to be the imaginings of one late-first-century writer (in Revelation) and the belief that the material of Jesus' physical body was transformed to leave the empty tomb. I have already indicated that the latter is at least debatable and the former can scarcely be evidence. So what is left is belief in the character of God as love and that God has taken at least one human being who was fully open to the divine presence into the divine life—the resurrection and ascen-

wm. James

---

4. See A. C. Thiselton in D. Fergusson and M. Sarot (eds.), *The Future as God's Gift*, T & T Clark, 2000, pp. 9-10.

sion of Jesus. Is not all the rest of Christian eschatology but empty speculation?[5]

While I respect the scrupulosity that prompts Peacocke's highly reserved approach, I believe his stance to be mistaken. We both share the conviction that trust in the God of love is the only ground for human expectation of a destiny beyond death, but I believe that it is necessary and possible to enquire more closely and specifically into how that steadfast love has been, and will be, acted out in history and beyond history. In the course of this exercise one may hope to gain some insight into the 'cash value' of a phrase such as the new heaven and the new earth. Some speculation is certainly involved — just as it is in some of the detailed prognostications of the physical cosmologists — but I do not believe that this is an 'empty' exercise. Rather it is one that is filled with Christian experience, insight and hope. In both science and theology, our anticipations of the future are influenced by our understandings of the past and present.

The Introduction to *Ends* concludes with a statement of the authors' stance and intent: 'The writers of this book share a common faith in a faithful Creator, a merciful Redeemer and a sanctifying Spirit. They believe that it is of the highest importance that Christians and the Christian church should not lose nerve in witnessing to our generation about the eschatological hope that is before us. They offer this book as a resource toward that end'.[6] It is in the same spirit, and with the same intent in mind, that I offer this slimmer volume.

5. A. R. Peacocke, *Zygon* 35 (2000), p. 135.
6. *Ends*, p. 13.

I

Scientific

and

Cultural Prologue

CHAPTER ONE

Cosmic Process: Past and Future

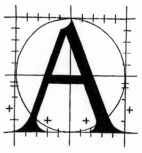s a prologue to our theological consideration of eschatology, we shall see what resources are available to us from culture in general and from science in particular. Because what is to come is related to what has been, we shall begin by considering science's account of the cosmic past and then its prognostications of the cosmic future.

EVOLVING FRUITFULNESS

The universe as we know it today emerged from the fiery singularity of the big bang, some fifteen billion years ago. Initially that world was extremely simple, being no more than an almost uniform expanding ball of energy. In the course of its long evolutionary history, the universe has become structured and diversified to a very high degree. The first generation of stars and galaxies condensed through the effects of gravity, which enhanced the small fluctuations of density present in the initial state of the cosmos. Within the interior nuclear furnaces of these first generation stars, many new chemical elements were formed, supplementing the hydrogen and helium that had constituted the primordial matter of the cosmos after the first three minutes of its bewilderingly rapid transformations of matter/energy. These chemical raw materials were then scattered abroad, and further augmented in their variety, through the effect of supernova explosions. When a second generation of stars and planets came into being, there was then available the appropriate chemical context within which carbon-based life could develop, here on Earth and perhaps on many other planets. Eventually the shuffling explorations of potentiality working through terrestrial biological evolution led to the appearance of self-conscious beings, the most astonishing development that we know about in all those fifteen billion years of cosmic history. In humanity, the universe had become aware of itself. As a corollary, science became a possibility, so that we are able to tell the story of our origins within the long history of the universe.

Although the universe appears to have been lifeless for the first eleven billion years of its existence, there is a real sense in which it was pregnant with the possibility of life from the very beginning. Only because the balance between the fundamental forces of gravity and electromagnetism is what it is and no different, have stars been able to burn for the billions of years that are necessary if they are to be able to fuel the development of life on one of their planets. Only because the laws of nuclear physics are what they are and no different, has the range of chemical elements necessary for carbon-based life been produced by the stars, from whose dead ashes we and

we are stardust

all other living creatures here on Earth are made. This remarkable collection of scientific insights into the 'finely tuned'
specificity of a biologically generative universe has been called
the Anthropic Principle.[1] Of course, it is the generality of
carbon-based life rather than the particularity of *homo sapiens*
that is the real concern of the Principle.

Evolutionary history seems to unfold through the interplay of two contrasting tendencies: 'chance' (by which is
meant the particularity of historical contingency, that this
happens rather than that), and 'necessity' (by which is meant
the generality of the lawfully regular environment within
which the process is played out, the reliability of the world).
No one supposes that the early universe was pregnant with the
genus *homo*, but if natural necessity had not taken the form it
actually does, then the chance explorations of contingent possibility would have been quite unable of themselves to bring
about the fruitfulness of life as we know it. There would have
been no carbon-based life because there would have been no
carbon.

The scientific facts on which the Anthropic Principle is
based are not open to doubt. Much contention, however, relates to what deeper metaphysical significance might or might
not be attributed to these remarkable insights.[2] Such finely
tuned potentiality might be held to indicate that there was a
purpose being fulfilled in cosmic history, but those who (like
the author) take that view have to be prepared to consider a

1. J. D. Barrow and F. J. Tipler, *The Anthropic Cosmological Principle*, Oxford
University Press, 1986; J. Leslie, *Universes*, Routledge, 1989.

2. Barrow and Tipler, *Anthropic Cosmological Principle*; Leslie, *Universes;* and
J. C. Polkinghorne, *Reason and Reality*, SPCK/Trinity Press International, 1991,
ch. 6.

number of other scientific insights of a rather different character, relating both to past events and to future expectations.

THREAT

Sixty-five million years ago an asteroid at least ten kilometres in diameter struck the Earth. The hundred million megatons of energy generated by its impact brought about catastrophic consequences for the terrestrial environment, eliminating the dinosaurs which for more than one hundred and fifty million years had dominated life on Earth. Thereby the little furry mammals, who are our ancestors, were given their evolutionary opportunity. Here was 'chance' operating on a grand scale to influence the development of life.

Events of this magnitude may be expected to occur on average at intervals of the order of a hundred million years. Lesser, but still very destructive, incidents occur more frequently. In 1908 a meteorite only fifty metres or so in diameter exploded over a remote region of Siberia, devastating an area at least two thousand square kilometres in extent. Had the explosion occurred over a big city, all of it would have been destroyed. Very considerable technological effort and accuracy would be needed to provide artificial protection against the recurrence of catastrophes of even this more limited and localised kind. In 1994 watchers on our planet were given a ringside seat to observe the kind of consequences that could flow from a collision with circulating debris. Over a period of six days, twenty-one fragments of comet Shoemaker-Levy 9 crashed into Jupiter. None was larger than seven hundred metres in diameter, but they produced scars on the Jovian atmosphere some of which were larger than the size of the Earth and which persisted for more than a year. The solar system is a dangerous environment, full of threats.

Other external dangers to our life on Earth, unpredictable in their onset, could arise from distant events such as a supernova explosion in our part of the galaxy, or the collision of two neutron stars to form a black hole. Either occurrence could deluge our planet with highly damaging radiation. Perhaps we give comparatively little attention to these external threats because of their largely unpredictable character and because the timescales within which they are likely to happen are very long compared with a human generation, or even with recorded human history.

Further threats to life originate within the planet itself, for example from viral or bacterial mutations, of which the impact of the HIV virus is an anticipatory experience. Some can arise from human hubris or carelessness, as anxieties about nuclear war and global pollution illustrate clearly enough. The continuing increase of the world's population serves to enhance the likelihood of disasters of this latter kind.

Many of these home-grown catastrophes could be very destructive but it is unlikely that they would wipe out human or animal life completely. However that life itself, in its intrinsic nature, is not inherently stable, for the average biological lifetime of a species is only a few million years before evolution may be expected to produce its successor. It is hard to know what this general fact implies for the future of human life, for in our case the ordinary Darwinian process has been considerably modified by the Lamarckian process of cultural evolution. The human power to transmit acquired knowledge across the generations is much more effective than the slow and uncertain process of the natural selection of genetic variations. In just a few thousands of years, the effects of human cultural development have produced enormous consequences for the terrestrial environment and for other species. Humanity now stands at the threshold of being able to intervene directly in the process of life itself, through the ambiguous powers conferred upon it by advances in genetic engineering.

The incidence of these threats is largely uncertain in its detail but, on a statistical basis, we can say that some are likely to occur eventually. The fact that life has survived on Earth for between three and four billion years, despite at least five major mass extinctions to which the fossil record testifies, shows that there is a certain resilience present in carbon-based life as a whole. However, there are further kinds of catastrophe that are certain to occur and which will be absolutely destructive in their consequences.

CERTAIN CATASTROPHES

The Sun shines through the effects of its internal nuclear reactions turning its hydrogen into helium. In about five billion years time, all the core hydrogen will be exhausted and the Sun will then swell to become a red giant, burning any life surviving on Earth into a frazzle in the process. Our understanding of the course of stellar evolution is good enough to make this prediction absolutely reliable.

Of course, by then it is possible that terrestrial life will have migrated elsewhere in the galaxy. However, the universe itself faces a highly problematic future. Its long-term history is controlled by the competing effects of expansion (the 'explosive' consequences of the big bang) and gravity (drawing matter together). These contrasting tendencies are very evenly balanced and we do not know for certain which will win in the end. If expansion predominates (the possibility currently favoured by most cosmologists), cosmic history will continue for ever in a world growing steadily colder and more dilute. Eventually, all will decay into low grade radiation. If gravity predominates, the present expansion will one day be halted and reversed. What began with the big bang will end with the big crunch, as the universe implodes into a cosmic melting pot. The timescales for these processes are immensely long, spanning many tens of billions of years, but one or other of them is a certain prognostication of the cosmic future. However fruitful the universe may seem today, its end lies in futility. It is perhaps not surprising that the distinguished American theoretical physicist Steven Weinberg, writing within the limited horizon of an atheist physicalism and with science alone as his guide, could say that the more he understood the universe, the more it seemed to him to be pointless.[3] Here is a challenge to which theology must respond. As William Stoeger says, 'if we are to take the truth discovered by the sciences seriously, denying the scientific description of death and the more reliably supported accounts of eventual life-ending and earth-ending catastrophes is really not an option'.[4]

QUESTIONS TO THEOLOGY

Jewish and Christian thinking takes seriously the reiterated divine statements in Genesis 1 that creation is 'good'. Although this claim is supported by science's discernment of the ratio-

3. S. Weinberg, *The First Three Minutes*, A. Deutsch, 1977, p. 143.
4. W. Stoeger, *Ends*, p. 19.

nal beauty and fruitful history of the universe, this goodness seems significantly qualified by the catastrophes and ultimate futility that we have been considering. Theology must negotiate these issues carefully. On the one hand, it would deny the reality of the present world as God's creation if it relied solely on 'pie in the sky' to come, yet, on the other hand, its account is incomplete on its own terms if it does not also point to a credible future hope beyond the demise of this universe.

Undoubtedly, in contemporary Western society, the most immediate threat to religious belief in an ultimately hopeful future is felt to lie not in the longer-term global threats we have been discussing, but in the short-term prospect of certain individual death, together with the widely held view that it results in the annihilation of the person. Of itself, science can only speak of presently embodied life and from its own resources it does not offer grounds for believing in the continuation of that life beyond the death of the body. To neuroscience, the mind appears to be ineluctably linked with the brain and so expected to perish with its decay. We shall see subsequently that Christian theology can fully accept a psychosomatic understanding of the human being, but it does not accept the further implications that are drawn from this by an atheistic style of thinking. That is because theology bases its post mortem hope on a reality inaccessible to scientific investigation, the faithfulness of the living God. In a similar way, theology can accept science's insight that an evolving world is one in which death is the necessary cost of new life, without thereby being condemned to supposing that the present process of the world represents the only form that the divine creative power might sustain in being. These issues await our later consideration. Meanwhile, we return to the significance of the catastrophes described in this chapter.

The spatial scale of much theological thinking is terrestrial, its timescale that of human history. Yet theology's real concern must be able to embrace the whole of created reality and the totality of cosmic history. In retrospect, in relation to the doctrine of creation, this has become widely acknowledged. Prospectively, in relation to eschatological fulfilment, there has been less extensive acceptance of all that this entails. But, if we are concerned with questions of ultimate significance, we cannot restrict ourselves to the domesticated horizon of simple human recollection and human expectation. The importance of the fact of cosmic collapse or decay is not diminished by its being so many billions of years in the future.

The gloomy prognostications of scientific cosmology press upon theology the necessity to recognise the seriousness of future threats and the vast timescales over which they operate. Whatever hopes there might be of human progress within history, they can amount to no more than a stay of execution of a sentence of inevitable futility. It is clear that a kind of evolutionary optimism that seeks a lasting fulfilment within the unfolding process of the present world is just not possible for us. Heraclitus was right, and all is in a state of flux. 'In our world, the cost of the evolution of novelty is the certainty of its impermanence'.[5] Not only is this true of species, but it is true also of the whole of carbon-based life, everywhere it may come to exist. Eventually it will prove only to have been a transient episode in cosmic history. As far as science is right in describing the future as the extrapolation of the past and present, the

5. J. C. Polkinghorne, *Ends*, p. 39.

world will certainly not end in the attainment of some climactic Ω point,[6] but in the whimper of cold decay or the bang of fiery collapse. An old-fashioned eschatology had as one of its slogans *Endzeit* is *Urzeit*, envisaging fulfilment as the restoration of a paradisal beginning that had been marred by the primeval disaster of the Fall. Ironically, a contemporary scientific cosmology could adopt the same slogan, but with the pessimistic prediction that the fire of the big bang will be mirrored by the fire of the big crunch.

'As far as science is right in describing the future . . . .' But theology claims that what is ultimate is not physical process but the will and purpose of God the Creator. God's final intentions will no more be frustrated by cosmic death on a timescale of tens of billions of years than they are by human death on a timescale of tens of years. The ultimate future does not belong to scientific extrapolation but to divine faithfulness. The credibility and meaning of that claim was the subject of the project conducted at the Center of Theological Inquiry at Princeton, which led to the publication of *The End of the World and the Ends of God*. As we have already noted, a persistent theme in that enquiry, and one which will also undergird the discussion of this book, was that a credible eschatological hope must involve both *continuity and discontinuity*. Without an element of continuity there is no real hope being expressed for this creation beyond its death; without an element of discontinuity, the prospect would be that of the non-hope of mere unending repetition. While it is for theology to say what it can about the 'new' that God will bring into being, if that new is to be understood as the eschatological transformation of the old,

6. Cf. P. Teilhard de Chardin, *The Phenomenon of Man*, Collins, 1959.

then science may have some modest role to play in clarifying what will be the necessary degree of continuity required for this to be the case. We must now consider what insights the natural sciences might have to offer to eschatological thinking in this way.

CHAPTER TWO

Insights from Natural Science

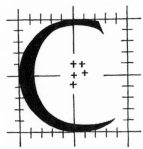ERTAIN general features characterise our understanding of the nature and history of the present physical universe. If that universe is rightly understood as being a divine creation, we may see these characteristics as being pale but true reflections of the will of the Creator. In that case, one might expect that the eschatological continuity between old and new would preserve these properties in some appropriate way.

FEATURES OF THE PRESENT CREATION

Among aspects thus to be considered are process; relationality; information; and mathematics.

Process
We have already sketched the evolutionary history of the universe and of life on Earth. Through the intricate unfolding

of physical process, initial simplicity has generated immense complexity. Theologically one can understand this complexity as the result of creation's having been endowed by its Creator with a profound potentiality which it has then been allowed to explore and realise as it 'makes itself'. God is not the tyrannical puppeteer of the universe, pulling every string so that all must dance to the divine tune alone, but rather the Creator is the God whose nature of love is patient and subtle, content to achieve the divine purposes in an open and developing way, in which the creatures themselves collaborate.[1] If that is the case for this present world, one may expect that similar characteristics will persist in appropriate ways as expressions of God's will for creation's destiny beyond its death. In other words, eschatological discontinuity will not be so abrupt as to be an apocalyptic abolition of the old, wiping the cosmic slate clean in an act of almost magical tour de force and so severing all connection between the old and the new — any more than the present creation came into being ready-made and fully formed, out of nothing at a snap of the divine fingers. There must be sufficient continuity for the new to be seen to arise *ex vetere*,[2] out of the old, as the latter's redemption from futility. Yet there must also be enough discontinuity so that the new is not just a repetition of the old, as if it were just a further turning of the evolutionary wheel of change brought about through death and decay.

This universe is a world of temporal process and, if we believe in the consistency of the divine Creator, we should not expect that its successor will be so radically different that it

---

1. J. C. Polkinghorne (ed.), *The Work of Love*, SPCK/Eerdmans, 2001.
2. J. C. Polkinghorne, *Science and Christian Belief/The Faith of a Physicist*, SPCK/Princeton University Press, 1996, ch. 9.

is, by contrast, a world of timeless existence. It too will surely have its developing history, though a history characterised by persisting fulfilment rather than transient coming-to-be.

Taking scientific insight seriously encourages reflections of this kind. Later we shall have to see how theology is able to respond to the challenges they present.

Relationality

Newtonian science pictured the motions of individual atoms as taking place within the 'container' of absolute space and in the course of the unfolding of absolute time. Modern physics has totally replaced this picture with something altogether more holistic and relational. Einstein's great discovery of general relativity tied together space, time and matter in a single physical package. Matter curves spacetime and the curvature of spacetime deflects the paths of matter. Thinking about them has to take a fully integrated form.

Quantum theory has shown that once two subatomic entities have interacted with each other, they remain mutually entangled, constituting effectively a single system, however far apart they may separate. Each retains a counter-intuitive power to influence the other instantaneously. This togetherness-in-separation, or non-locality, is called the EPR effect,[3] and some beautiful experiments have verified it as a property of nature. It appears that even the subatomic world cannot properly be treated atomistically.

At the more everyday level of macroscopic phenomena, chaos theory has revealed the widespread existence of sys-

3. See, for example, J. C. Polkinghorne, *The Quantum World*, Longman/ Princeton University Press, 1984, ch. 7.

tems exquisitely sensitive to the finest details of their circumstances, and this implies that entities of this kind can never be treated in isolation from the effects of their environment. The slightest nudge will totally change their future behaviour. In all these ways, a methodologically reductionist science has learned that physical reality cannot adequately be treated atomistically.

Such insights are congenial to Christian theology, the nature of whose triune God is founded in the relational exchange (*perichoresis*, as the theologians call it) between the Persons of the Holy Trinity. For eschatological thinking, this emphasis on relationality implies the inadequacy of a purely individual concept of human destiny. In connection with the human community, this insight has frequently been accepted. Yet in connection with humanity considered in relation to the rest of creation, this has been less widely acknowledged, for much theological thinking has been unduly anthropocentric in its focus, regarding the remainder of creation as being little more than a backdrop before which the human drama is being played out.

Information

The science of the twenty-first century is likely to concern itself to a significant extent with an increasing understanding of the properties of complex systems. So far little has been possible beyond the study of certain computerised models of networks of moderate complexity. Already, however, this 'natural history' encounter with specific instances has raised expectations of very significant discoveries awaiting those who will be able to penetrate beneath particular behaviour to discern the deeper theory that undoubtedly underlies the striking phenomena displayed by the individual cases so far studied. Most impressive has been the capacity of such systems spontaneously to generate very considerable patterns of ordered behaviour.

The kind of effects concerned can be illustrated by a system studied by Stuart Kauffman.[4] A physical realisation of his computer model would consist of a large array of light bulbs, each of which has its behaviour of being on or off correlated with the behaviours of two other bulbs somewhere in the array. If they are both on, it is more likely to be on also at the next step of the system's development. If the system is started off in some random configuration, with some bulbs on and some bulbs off, and then allowed to develop according to these rules, instead of just flickering away haphazardly for ever, the system soon settles down to cycling through a very limited number of particular on/off patterns. This unexpected behaviour represents the generation of an astonishing degree of overall orderliness. If there are 10,000 light bulbs in the array, there are about 10^{3000} possible configurations that might in principle occur. In practice, however, the system cycles through only about 100!

This remarkable generation of order out of chaos strongly suggests that if the behaviour of complex systems is to be described and understood adequately, this task will call not only for the conventional 'bits and pieces' account in terms of the interactions of constituents but also for a complementary holistic account in terms of the overall pattern of the whole. In scientific terms, one can say that the conventional picture of

4. S. Kauffman, *At Home in the Universe*, Oxford University Press, 1995, ch. 4.

energetic exchanges between particles will need to be supplemented by a description of the whole, framed in terms of the effects of information generation (that is to say, the specification of complex pattern).[5]

We see here the prospect of the revival of an antique notion, reclothed in modern dress. Aristotle had spoken of both matter (*hyle*) and form (*eidos*). We are just beginning to learn how to speak, in a parallel way, about energy and information. Just as Thomas Aquinas used the revived Aristotelian science of his day as an aid to his theological thinking, so we, in our time, may find theological value in making use of the analogical resource that these scientific developments offer us. In pursuit of our present eschatological task, we shall see later that this method may be of particular relevance to how we may understand the nature of the human soul.

Mathematics

Mathematics is the natural language of science. Fundamental physics, we have discovered, is always expressed in beautiful equations.[6] In itself, that is quite a striking fact about the universe, and the deep intelligibility and rational beauty that it

5. Important issues will require further clarification as these ideas develop. For the use of the language of information/pattern to be appropriate, the results of process should not only be highly improbable but also exhibit some kind of specifiable order. Tricky problems of interpretation can be involved. A long string of letters in an unintelligible arrangement is as a priori improbable as a string of equal length making an intelligible sentence, but the former might also convey information, and embody a pattern, if it were in a code to which one possessed the key. Discussions of some of the relevant issues, which were developed for different reasons and in very different contexts, can be found in P. Davies, *The Mind of God*, Simon and Schuster, 1992, ch. 5; W. A. Dembski, *Intelligent Design*, IVP, 1999, chs. 5 and 6.

6. J. C. Polkinghorne, *Beyond Science*, Cambridge University Press, 1996, pp. 79-80.

expresses have been seen as providing the basis for a revived and insightful kind of natural theology.[7] A world shot through with such signs of mind may well be thought to reflect the Mind of its Creator.

Yet, what is mathematics itself? Its practitioners resist the suggestion that it is a constructive form of intellectual play. They believe that their researches are true discoveries, explorations of an already-existing reality.[8] The prime numbers and the Mandelbrot set have always been 'there'. But 'where' have they been? If these convictions of the mathematicians are correct (as I believe them to be), then in addition to the physical world that the scientists investigate, there must be an everlasting noetic world of mathematical entities that the mathematicians investigate. These worlds may be thought of as being in some kind of complementary relationship with each other.[9] Together they constitute dimensions of created reality.

These ideas are obliquely relevant to our central concern. Their principal consequence for our present purposes would be the enabling of an enlargement of the ontological imagination, arising from within science itself broadly construed, rather than from explicit considerations of a religious character. Once arguments of this kind have encouraged the thought that there might be more things in heaven and earth than can be accounted for by conventional scientific thinking, then the extra noetic dimension thus introduced into reality can also be seen, in a platonic fashion, as affording a lodging for those

7. See J. C. Polkinghorne, *Science and Creation*, SPCK, 1988, chs. 1 and 2.
8. J. C. Polkinghorne, *Belief in God in an Age of Science*, Yale University Press, 1998, ch. 6.
9. Polkinghorne, *Science and Creation*, ch. 5; *Faith, Science and Understanding*, SPCK/Yale University Press, 2000, ch. 5.4.

powerful ideas of goodness and beauty that likewise seem to transcend notions of their being mere human contrivances. If there are elements of reality beyond the flux of time, then there might also be a destiny beyond the temporal ending of this world.

RESPONSES WITHIN SCIENCE

The universal futility that cosmology predicts as the world's fate has elicited a number of responses from scientists who are unwilling to look to religion for the possibility of a wider prospect beyond the end of physical process. These reactions have included defiance; a total view; 'physical eschatology'; and endless fertility.

Defiance

According to this point of view, the only fitting attitude is a stoic defiance in the face of threatened futility. All culture, including science, will be no more than a transient episode, but while human society lasts it represents a small island of self-created meaning, around which laps the ocean of cosmic meaninglessness. It was in this spirit that Weinberg wrote: 'The effort to understand the universe is one of the very few things that lifts human life a little above the level of farce and gives it some of the grace of tragedy'.[10] This pessimistic view is not without its own austere nobility. It makes it very clear what is at stake in the discussion of eschatological issues. Far from being matters of mere speculation about vastly distant events, their concern is whether the universe is ultimately a cosmos or a chaos, a world whose history makes total sense

10. S. Weinberg, *The First Three Minutes*, A. Deutsch, 1977, p. 143.

or a world whose history is just a concatenation of one thing after another, a 'tale told by an idiot, full of sound and fury, signifying nothing', as Macbeth said.

A Total View

While the universe may end badly, perhaps it is to the complete sweep of cosmic history, considered as a whole from beginning to end, that we should look if we wish to discern its significance. Meaning is to be found in the whole process and not in individual events. Such an attitude would be reinforced if it were true, as some believe, that it is the atemporal entity of the whole spacetime continuum that is the true reality, and our impression that we participate in a moving historic present is a trick of human psychological perspective. This so-called 'block universe' account is often defended on two grounds said to be derived from science:[11] the failure of the equations of physics to accommodate the concept of 'now', and a claim that the fact that special relativity implies that differently moving observers make different judgements about the simultaneity of distant events shows that the distinction between past, present and future is an illusion. I do not believe that either of these arguments works. If physics fails to describe the present moment, so much the worse for physics. Its inability to include this fundamental aspect of human encounter with the world should be seen as doing no more than indicating the narrow limits of a purely physicalist understanding, rather than disposing of a basic human experience. As for relativity theory, observers' judgements about the temporal ordering of distant

11. C. J. Isham and J. C. Polkinghorne, 'The Debate over the Block Universe', in R. J. Russell, N. Murphy and C. J. Isham (eds.), *Quantum Cosmology and the Laws of Nature*, Vatican Observatory, 1993, pp. 135-44.

events are always unambiguously *retrospective* (since signals about them can only be received when they are within the observer's backward lightcone), and so this can do nothing to establish the pre-existent reality of the future.

Nevertheless, Albert Einstein seems to have embraced the notion of the block universe. When his great friend Michele Besso died, Einstein wrote what was clearly intended to be a consolatory letter to his widow. In it, he said, 'Now he has departed a little ahead of me from this quaint world. This means nothing. For us faithful physicists, the separation between past, present and future has only the meaning of an illusion, though a persistent one'.[12]

The concept of an atemporally existent lifespan (one's personal world-line, one might say in scientific terms) is the scientific equivalent of process theology's idea of objective immortality,[13] our complete life held in the memory of God. Both these ways of looking at human significance fall far short of total meaningfulness, for they relate simply to static preservation of what has been (including all its incompletenesses and frustrations and, a theologian would wish to say, its sinfulness) and they do not offer the hope of a dynamic fulfilment (in the course of which unfinished business is completed and hurts are healed and sins forgiven).

'Physical Eschatology'

While carbon-based life can have only a finite timespan, once intelligence has come into being in this way, maybe it will re-engineer its embodiment so as to preserve its activity how-

---

12. Quoted in M. Jammer, *Einstein and Religion*, Princeton University Press, 1999, p. 161.

13. See I. G. Barbour, *Religion and Science*, SCM Press, 1998, p. 304.

ever cosmic circumstances change. Advocates of a strong view of artificial intelligence believe that we are close to seeing this happen with the emergence of primitive forms of silicon-based 'life'.

Freeman Dyson has considered the case of a continually expanding universe, in which he believes that information-processing could continue indefinitely, albeit at ever slower rates and in large physical systems that would have to husband their dwindling energy supplies through enduring long periods of dormancy.[14] Obviously, this scheme offers no future hope for humanity beyond the demise of carbon-based life. However, a much more ambitious proposal for another kind of physical eschatology has come from Frank Tipler.[15] He considers the case of a collapsing universe, which he believes could be manipulated so that its final phase would correspond to the whole cosmos becoming an ever-faster racing computer, fueled by the shear energy of the collapse and capable of processing an infinite amount of information in its dying gasp. In a curious echo of Teilhard de Chardin, Tipler calls this ultimate cosmic computer Omega, regarding it as constituting a 'physical god'. He even believes that Ω would 'resurrect' human beings by creating computer emulations of them in the course of its final highly energetic phase. Tipler shows himself to be a kind of 'Southern Baptist atheist', as he seeks through his 'physical eschatology' to recapture and reconceive the language of old time religion, now translated into purely physicalist terms.

As an imaginative exercise, Tipler's proposal is some-

14. F. J. Dyson, *Infinite in Both Directions*, Harper and Row, 1988, ch. 6.
15. F. J. Tipler, *The Physics of Immortality*, Macmillan, 1994.

thing of a tour de force. As a serious eschatological proposition, it is highly unconvincing. Many objections can be made to it. We have good reasons to believe that human beings are much more than finite state machines ('computers made of meat'),[16] so that the idea of resurrection through emulation (computer modelling) is not a coherent expectation. In any case, why should Omega be expected to be concerned with humanity? Tipler displays breathtaking boldness in the assumptions he is willing to make about the behaviour of matter in regimes very distant indeed from any of which we could claim to have sober scientific knowledge. Those bold speculators who talk about the very early universe have to make guesses about physical behaviour about 10^{-43} seconds after the big bang; Tipler is willing to guess behaviour $10^{-10^{10}}$ seconds away from the big crunch.

When the efforts of physical eschatology are properly evaluated, they seem simply to confirm our previous verdict that the physical process of this present universe can end only in futility. In this connection it is instructive to compare Tipler with Teilhard de Chardin,[17] who also presents a picture of unfolding fulfilment within present process. Yet Teilhard's vision of the end is not computerisation but christogenesis; the inspiration of his thought is not physicalist but eucharistic. Christoph Schwöbel comments, 'It is this reference to the evolution of Christ which, before the eschaton, is

16. R. Penrose, *The Emperor's New Mind*, Oxford University Press, 1989, ch. 10; J. Searle, *Minds, Brains and Science*, BBC Publications, 1984; *The Rediscovery of the Mind*, MIT Press, 1992, ch. 2. In *Ends* (p. 42), Detlev Linke makes this point by drawing attention to the many timescales present in the brain, in contrast to the single standard clock of a computer.

17. P. Teilhard de Chardin, *The Divine Milieu*, Harper, 1960.

pre-actualised in holy communion which prevents Teilhard's thought from becoming pantheistic'.[18] Tipler, on the other hand, devises the scenario of a sort of evolving pantheism. One may feel, as I do, that Teilhard concedes too much to the hopes of a kind of evolutionary optimism and that he takes too little account of scientific predictions of cosmic futility, but at least he rests his thinking on a credible theistic basis.

Endless Fertility

There are scientists who are endeavouring to apply quantum theory to the whole universe, despite our current ignorance of how to combine quantum theory and general relativity into the single account that would be needed for a true quantum cosmology.[19] Speculations of this kind are interesting but uncertain and not much should be built upon them. Yet one proposal is of some interest for our present concern. It supposes that baby universes are continually bubbling up from fluctuations in the primeval ur-state, which is the quantum gravitational vacuum. Many such bubbles just fade away, but some are blown up, by a process called inflation, into entities of cosmic dimensions, enjoying cosmic lifetimes. We are believed, by those who espouse this view, to be living in one such long-lived fluctuation. In the end our particular bubble will burst, but others 'elsewhere' will come into existence as its successors. The cosmic pot will boil away 'for ever'. Even if something like this proposal were to prove to be correct, it would

18. C. Schwöbel, 'Last Things First', in D. Fergusson and M. Sarot (eds.), *The Future as God's Gift*, T & T Clark, 2000, p. 234.

19. See C. J. Isham, 'Quantum Theories of the Creation of the Universe', in Russell et al. (eds.), *Quantum Cosmology*, pp. 49–89.

only present a scene of occasional islands of transient mean-ingfulness erupting within an ocean of absurdity.

From its own unaided resources, natural science can do no more than present us with the contrast of a finely tuned and fruitful universe which is condemned to ultimate futility. If that paradox is to receive a resolution, it will be beyond the reach of science on its own. We shall have to explore whether theology can take us further by being both humble enough to learn what it can from science and also bold enough to hold firm to its own sources of insight and understanding.

CHAPTER THREE

Human Intuition and Experience

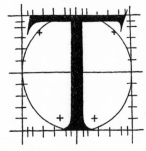 HE next part of our preliminary consideration must call upon the human sciences for help as it concerns itself with how individual human beings face the future and attend to the certainty of their deaths.

HOPE

In his contribution to *The End of the World and the Ends of God*, Fraser Watts approached issues of eschatology from the point of view of a psychologist.[1] His contribution contrasted propositional and attitudinal approaches to the subject. The former (characteristic, Watts believes, of the style of the natural sciences) has an 'objective' air to it as it discusses the nature of the last things. Its orientation is towards the future and its danger is that it can degenerate into mere optimism, a belief that future will prove to be 'all right', expressed in rigidly

1. F. W. Watts, *Ends*, ch. 4.

reified terms. The latter (characteristic of the human sciences) has a 'subjective' air, concerned as it is with the quality of life here and now. Its danger is that it can degenerate into mere fantasy about the present, expressed in vaguely spiritualised terms.

These two approaches relate to what the theologians call 'futurist eschatology' and 'realised eschatology', respectively. (As the names suggest, the one lays emphasis on a radical transformation that will take place at the end of present history, while the other centres upon the transformation of life now, within present history.) Watts is surely right to call for the holding of a balance between the two perspectives that he has identified, in the same way that many theologians seek an 'inaugurated eschatology', that retains elements of both realised and futurist eschatology in the tension of the already/not yet that is part of the Christian experience of salvation. Hope provides an important mediating concept. *proleptic*

Hope is carefully to be distinguished, on the one hand from optimism (which springs from prediction of what the future will bring), and on the other hand from wishful thinking (which is unconstrained by the probabilities of what that future might bring). Hope is based neither on certainty, as if it were simple extrapolation of the present, nor on fantasy, as if its object bore only a tenuous relation to the present. Once again, we encounter the eschatological dialectic of continuity and discontinuity. In relation to hope, failure to respect this balance can lead either to despair that anything will ever change for the better, or to violent imaginings of apocalyptic destruction in which the future can be attained only by the annihilation of the past. As Watts says, true hope 'thrives on a sense of what is inaugurated and possible, but always still coming into being'.[2] 'Now hope that is seen is not hope. For who hopes for what is seen?' (Romans 8:24). For the Christian, hope arises out of endurance in the face of adversity, based on trust in the love of God (Romans 5:3–5). Hope is essentially moral in its character, for it is a good future for which we may dare to hope. If that is the case, we should be prepared to work for what we hope for. Of course, human striving cannot bring about our ultimate destiny, for that lies in the hands of God, but spiritual formation can fit us for what that final destiny is hoped to be. Moreover, to the extent that hope is partially realisable within present history, it is a realisation that is to be striven for. As Jürgen Moltmann says of the theology of hope, it is 'a theology of combatants, and not of onlookers'.[3]

INTUITIONS OF REALITY

In facing the future, human beings face the certainty of death. No aspect of the limitation of human nature might seem more obvious than our mortality. 'Golden lads and lasses must, as chimney sweepers, come to dust' (Shakespeare, *Cymbeline*). Yet we also find within ourselves aspirations that point beyond the curtailment of death, that refuse to grant the last word to human finitude. 'Death be not proud. . . . Death thou shalt die' (John Donne). Humanity's sad restlessness at the thought of the necessary incompleteness of any life lived in this world, together with human defiance of the apparent finality of death, are intuitions that we should take seriously into account. The more positively expressed side of this stance is hope.

2. Watts, *Ends*, p. 51.
3. J. Moltmann, *The Coming of God*, SCM Press, 1996, p. 146.

Despite the strangeness, bitterness, incompleteness of this present life, human beings frequently do not give way to despair. In the human heart there is something that corresponds to the conviction expressed so powerfully by the great fourteenth-century mystic, Mother Julian of Norwich, that in the end 'all shall be well and all manner of things shall be well'. I believe that this intuition of hope is a significant and essential aspect of what it is to be human. It is not just a survival technique for whistling in the dark to keep our spirits up, but it is an encounter with the reality within which we live.

The sociologist of religion, Peter Berger, draws our attention to this phenomenon in his marvellous little book, *A Rumour of Angels*.[4] Its concern is with everyday occurrences which, when we stop to think about what they actually mean, point us beyond the everyday to a more profound encounter with reality. Berger calls these happenings 'signals of transcendence'. One of them is this: A child wakes in the night, frightened by a bad dream. A parent goes to comfort the child, saying 'It's all right'. Berger asks us to consider what is going on here. Is the parent uttering a loving lie about this world of cancer and concentration camps? Or is the parent conveying to the child a deep understanding of reality—all those other things notwithstanding—that is an essential component in the child's process of growing into human maturity? Berger believes it is the latter, and so do I. Human beings possess a significant intuition that in the end all shall be well.

We may find a surprising confirmation of this deep-seated feeling of hope where one might not have expected to look for it, in the writings of a number of twentieth-century Ger-

4. P. Berger, *A Rumour of Angels*, Penguin, 1970.

man Marxist philosophers. Although their words are somewhat dark and obscured, they are not without a glimmer of hope. Ernst Bloch could write that 'wherever existence draws near to its kernel [that is, the central reality of human existence], continuance begins—not as a petrified continuance but one that holds within itself the *Novum* without transience, without corruptibility'.[5] Max Horkheimer expressed the longing present in the human heart, that the murderer should not triumph over his innocent victim. Theodor Adorno found the idea of the finality of death to be 'unthinkable'.

In *The End of the World and the Ends of God*, Larry Bouchard considered how certain kinds of science fiction explore a future scenario of both fragmentation and restoration,[6] a theme whose hopefulness is Pelagian in its reliance on the power of human effort and technical manipulation. The authors discussed know that 'while Earth is our cradle, it cannot be forever home'. Bouchard's Christian comment is 'that the cosmos will be slave to us is impossible; that we and the cosmos can be servants to each other is conceivable; that God will enter the suffering of slaves and servants and lift up their lives into God is what is promised'.[7]

Michael Pafford culled from literature and autobiography accounts of what he calls 'unattended moments'[8] More personal and individual than Berger's signals of transcendence, these testimonies share with them the character of affording access to a deeper dimension of reality than is readily perceptible in the generality of daily life. After a quotation

5. Quoted in Moltmann, *Coming of God*, p. 64.
6. L. Bouchard, *Ends*, ch. 7.
7. Ibid., p. 105.
8. M. Pafford, *The Unattended Moment*, SCM Press, 1976.

from Forrest Reid, who had a profound experience of beauty and goodness in a country churchyard, Pafford comments,

> The place was beautiful and made him feel good but who shall say what beauty and goodness are? Did his eye make the churchyard beautiful or the churchyard make him good? Because the unattended moment is unitive it heals those harmful divisions into which the speculative mind of man forever tends to polarise the wholeness of experience. Both the object and the subject were compounded of innocence, which is freedom from association with guilt and sin, simplicity which is freedom from confusion and complexity, peace which is freedom from noise and from restless thoughts and impulses.[9]

Such experiences are not always hopeful, but often they are. Another of Pafford's witnesses described the feeling of 'absolute freedom from mortality, accompanied by an indescribable calm and joy'[10]

Alister Hardy accumulated an extensive archive of spiritual experiences reported by people less professionally articulate than the members of the literary world.[11] Surveys showed that these experiences were much more common than many would suppose. One of Hardy's contributers wrote,

> The eternal nature of God as perfect love filled me with an inexpressible sense of joy and complete reassurance that above all our storms is tranquillity and wholeness. I now know that anxiety has no place, and discouragement cannot be more than a temporary setback. In face of this, what can one do but worship? It adds a new dimension to 'living in hope'[12]

9. Ibid., p. 86.
10. Ibid., p. 88.
11. A. Hardy, *The Spiritual Nature of Man*, Oxford University Press, 1979.
12. Ibid., p. 62.

While these kinds of experience are certainly not universal, they are sufficiently widespread to count as an element in the human encounter with reality that demands to be considered with utmost seriousness. They are intuitions of a realm not bounded by the horizon of death. It is significant that many of the people who report insightful occasions of this kind are not religious believers in any conventional sense and so by no means do they always feel the need to use religious phraseology in the way that the witness quoted did. There seems to be a root human intuitive experience involved that lies deeper than cultural or cultic influences (though a theologian will, nevertheless, understand it as an experience of the veiled divine presence).

For many people, art provides the window through which they glimpse a sight of an everlasting reality underlying the flux of the changing world. Richard Bauckham has discussed the way in which artistic experience 'enables us to indwell the moment that otherwise escapes us', developing his theme in terms of an extensive analysis of insights derived from considering Virginia Woolf's *To the Lighthouse* and Claude Monet's famous sequence of paintings of the lily pond at Giverny.[13] Bauckham quotes a remark of John Berger that 'all the languages of art have been developed as an attempt to transform the instantaneous into the permanent'.[14] For Bauckham, representative art, operating in this way, affords us an image of how the divine act of new creation will transform the old creation into its everlasting destiny. Once again we encounter the human intuition that there is the hope of a reality beyond transience.

13. R. Bauckham, *God Will Be All in All*, T & T Clark, 1999, pp. 193–226.
14. Ibid., p. 194.

Considerations of a different kind relate to the stories that originate from people who have come back to life after apparently being clinically dead.[15] Clearly such people did not die biologically, and so their experiences are rightly characterised as being 'near death'. There are considerable commonalities in what they have to relate: a tunnel experience, leading to greeting by a figure of light and sensations of warmth and welcome, but then the order to return to this life, which is accepted with considerable reluctance. Often this is coupled with an experience of seeming to float above one's body.

It is hard to know what to make of these testimonies. Caution is certainly in order. The degree of unanimity may reflect no more than the common reaction of an anoxic brain in a moribund condition. Perhaps the most impressive thing about people who have had near death experiences of this kind, is the way in which they perceive them so positively, often leading to a complete lack of fear of the death that must eventually come to them in final reality.

Even more open to question are the claims of mediums to have contact with the dead.[16] Much fraud and self-delusion have clearly been involved in many of the cases reported, but there have been investigators who have felt that there is a residue of claims that are deserving of more respectful attention. Christian tradition, drawing on its Jewish roots (Leviticus 19:31), has looked askance at such activity. One must say that the frequent vagueness and banality of the messages claimed

---

15. See, for example, H. Kung, *Eternal Life?* Collins, 1984, ch. 1.
16. For a careful discussion, see J. Hick, *Death and Eternal Life*, Collins, 1976, pp. 129–46.

to be conveyed do not add cogency to taking these phenomena seriously.

Some of the unexpected knowledge said to be in the possession of mediums could be explained if they were in telepathic communication with the living persons consulting them. Telepathy is, perhaps, the paranormal phenomenon for which there seems to be the best testimony, perplexing though it is to science to conceive how such a form of communication could be possible. The philosopher H. H. Price appealed to telepathy, and to dream experiences, in order to defend the coherence of belief in the possibility of the existence of disembodied minds, and to speculate what their experiences might be like.[17] In this book we shall place no reliance on any paranormal phenomena and we shall take the view that it is intrinsic to full humanity to be embodied, in some way or another.

It seems likely that ever since the Neanderthals began to bury their dead in a fetal position (significant of new birth) and coloured with red ochre (significant of blood and new life), there has been some intuition that death is not the last word in relation to human destiny. The chapters ahead will explore what basis there might be for such an eschatological hope.

17. See ibid., pp. 265–70.

CHAPTER FOUR

Cultural Context

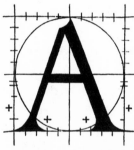 T the end of the nineteenth cen-
tury, A. R. Wallace (whose indepen-
dent discovery of the principle of
natural selection had finally prodded
Charles Darwin into publishing *Origin of Species*), wrote a book with the
title, *The Wonderful Century*. Richard
Bauckham and Trevor Hart, in their joint book about eschatology,[1] comment how unlikely it would have been for an
author writing at the end of the twentieth century to have
chosen a similar title. The deaths and devastations caused by
two world wars, and by many other bloody but more localised conflicts, have made that century one which has darkened
human expectations of the future. The Holocaust, and the
other terrible incidents of institutionalised persecution and
genocide that have punctuated the twentieth century, have

1. R. Bauckham and T. Hart, *Hope Against Hope*, Darton, Longman and
Todd, 1999.

37

shown the depravity of which human beings are capable when a social system enforcing a fearful obedience to the State induces many thousands to execute the evil will of their ruthless leaders. The Gulags, and the eventual collapse of the Soviet system, demonstrated the vanity of expecting a social utopia to be attained through a political agenda. The threats of nuclear war and global pollution, enhanced by rapid population increase, hang over the world as it enters the third millennium.

THE LEGACY OF THE PAST

Lecturing in Heidelberg before the First World War, Ernst Troeltsch could say that 'nowadays the eschatological bureau is closed most of the time',[2] but subsequent developments have forced it to reopen as people anxiously question whether there might yet be hope and meaningfulness to be found among the debris of history. Both the progressive optimism of the nineteenth century and the depressive experience of the twentieth century continue to shape our thinking about the future. Jürgen Moltmann places before us a challenge: 'Consciously or unconsciously, the eschatological thinking of the present day is determined by the messianic visions of the nineteenth century and the apocalyptic terrors experienced in the history of the twentieth century. What hope can be justified, once we wake up out of the messianic dreams and resist the apocalyptic anxieties?'[3]

The dreams turned into nightmares, thereby making resistance to the anxieties a yet more difficult task. An exter-

2. Quoted in D. Fergusson and M. Sarot (eds.), *The Future as God's Gift*, T & T Clark, 2000, p. 217.

3. J. Moltmann, *The Coming of God*, SCM Press, 1996, p. 5.

ministic mentality is present in contemporary society, chillingly illustrated by deeds of terrorism or suicide acted out by small extremist sects, and less dramatically, but still insidiously, exemplified by an obsession in films, literature and video games with scenarios of violent destruction. Inner fears are projected onto an external apocalypse. It seems as if, were there anything to hope for at all, it must lie the other side of some great global disaster.[4]

PRESENT CONSEQUENCES

Such a mood induces a withdrawal into the private self. A hopeful eschatology can then take only the existential form of some kind of inner fulfilment. This tendency is reinforced by a solipsistic individualism that supposes value to arise solely from privately made assessments. If there is no moral or aesthetic reality independent of ourselves, why should anything be expected to persist beyond our individual demise? If there is any form of hope, it will then centre on a wholly realised eschatology, for only in the present can one be certain of life at all. Religions that seek to counter this stance may, in response, find themselves being driven by contrast to an appeal to a wholly futurist eschatology, focussed on what lies beyond the apocalyptic destruction of this world. Yet such a 'pie in the sky' kind of hope is a distortion of Christian eschatology. Moltmann says that its denial of the value of the present moment amounts to a kind of 'religious atheism'.[5] In later chapters we shall have to explore how it is possible to build up a

4. Cf. L. Bouchard, *Ends*, ch. 7, which gives an extensive discussion using contemporary literature, and in particular Walter Miller's novel *Canticle for Liebowitz*, as a source of insight.
5. Moltmann, *Coming of God*, p. 50.

more balanced account of eschatological hope than is offered by either of these two extremes.

Emphasis on the present can induce the feeling of a frenetic need to grasp the immediate possibility, to live life with the motto *carpe diem* (seize the moment). William Schweiker writes that 'we live in a time obsessed world. Among advanced, late-modern societies the speed of travel and communication as well as production and consumption spells an unrelenting demand for instantaneous satisfaction of human desires and wants'.[6] Time is compressed by the closing in of the horizon of expectation, with its demand that technology should provide instant solutions to pressing human problems. Science's predictions of eventual catastrophe then both trouble the mind and yet also seem unreal to the present because of their remoteness. The middle ground between now and the end becomes lost to view.

If the present moment is all, then the succession of these moments must be made to continue for as long as possible. A kind of medical eschatology results, holding out the prospect of the unnatural prolongation of individual human lives. What previous generations had sought to achieve by the crude techniques of the injection of monkey glands is now held by some to be within our grasp through advances in genetics and in transplant medicine. The more extravagant versions of this myth imply that death may become optional, at least for the very rich. A grisly route to the same end is offered at lesser expense to those who choose to have their moribund bodies deep frozen, awaiting clinical developments that will cure their terminal disease when they are unfrozen again in the future. The

6. W. Schweiker, *Ends*, p. 124.

hollowness of such expedients is illustrated by the suggestion that if preserving the whole body seems too expensive an option, then at least the head might be frozen in the eventual hope of even more extraordinary medical advances.

A yet cheaper, and more widely accessible, strategy for grasping, or rather exceeding, the present moment might be afforded by the electronic illusions of cyberspace. They represent a way of offering a 'drive towards a world where experience and imagination become indistinguishable'.[7] Virtual reality is called in to compensate for the shortcomings of actual reality.

Common to all these recipes for personal fulfilment is a shallowness of content and a rejection of reality. Averting one's eyes from the prospect of death, whether personal or cosmic, does not thereby serve to abolish mortality. Nor does emphasis on the now remove the reality of the depth of time. It simply distances people from essential resources.

CULTURAL MEMORY

'Cultivation of *cultural memory* is displaced by the reinforced and demanding collective attention paid to the present and the near future'.[8] In actual fact no one can live quite so relentlessly contemporary a life. No one can escape wholly from the influence of their cultural context, and that involves them in a degree of inescapable linkage with previous generations. What such great emphasis on the present can do is to qualify and change the way in which the past is apprehended and experienced.

7. Polkinghorne and Welker, *Ends*, p. 10.
8. Ibid. p. 9.

Jan Assman[9] distinguished between cold memory and hot memory. The former reduces the past to a collection of bits of factual information, curious and interesting in their way but without contemporary influence. Cold memories of this kind are provided for us in abundance by books and television programmes that depict the strange way in which peoples behaved and believed in that distant country of the past.

Hot memory, on the contrary, is the way in which the past remains still active in the present. It carries into our generation the traditions and insights that formed a community whose life is spread out over history, and of which we are but the most recent members. At its best, hot memory does not imply a static antiquarian enthralment to the way things have always been done, but it offers dynamic participation in a still unfolding historical process, where the insights of the past are available as corrections to the limited perspectives of the present. One of the ways in which a cultural memory maintains its strength is through a textual canon whose compiling (as in the assembly of the materials of the Hebrew Bible over many centuries) and interpretation (as in the continuing Christian reflection on the deposit of the New Testament) intertwines the thought of many generations. The way in which the cultivation of cultural memory is being displaced in many communities today lies in a shaping and cooling of their recollections and in the rejection of the idea of canonical literature. Deconstructionism

Of course, not all the effects of hot memory are beneficial. The tribal loyalties and antagonisms that we see, for example, in the two communities in Northern Ireland, result

9. Ibid.

from a very heated recollection of the past. Yet some living relationship with history is necessary if we are to attain to a creative and realistically expectant relationship to the future. A thin past can give rise only to a thin future. There has to be a certain thickness in our engagement with time.

One expression of this experience of temporal depth is afforded by a rhythmic sensitivity to a life lived within the measures given us by succeeding generations, alternating seasons, the temporal mileposts of the liturgical year, the contrast of Sabbath and weekday, times of Jubilee with their release from past debt. These influences are much muted in contemporary society. Seven-day shopping and strawberries in season all the year round are tokens that this is so. Even the dawn of a new millennium does not amount to much more than an excuse for a good party and a firework show.

A prime method for the preservation of hot memory is through myth, those powerful stories of origin and ancestors that embody and perpetuate the self-understanding of a community. As memory cools, myth is replaced by metaphysics until that itself dissolves into a plurality of personal opinions. In our time, Jean-François Lyotard has proclaimed and celebrated a postmodern incredulity towards metanarratives, asserting the death of the overarching, meaningful story. The recovery of hot memory, and of the significance of time, will require a restored appropriation of the power of story to forge and express human identity and understanding. The meaning of stories lies in their endings, an insight that points to the significance of the future. The prevalence of 'happy endings' is not mere sentimentality, but an insight of eschatological hopefulness that in the end all shall be well.

A world obsessed by the present will have only cold memories of the past and apocalyptic fears for the future. It will be a world of multiple opinions and no shared stories, the setting for a skimpy and etiolated human existence which is a kind of life on half pay. A world of this kind is reminiscent of the lunar landscape portrayed by science, as a consequence of its self-chosen decision to concentrate on the impersonal aspects of our encounter with reality—a world populated by quarks and gluons but without persons in it, quantifiable but without value, condemned to ultimate cosmic futility. It is scarcely open to doubt that the modern mood has been greatly influenced by science's success and by what is perceived to be the character of scientific practice.[10]

Many people are disposed to believe that here is *the* method for gaining real knowledge and so they are inclined to set aside serious consideration of other forms of human search for understanding. Yet we need to recognise that science's considerable success has been purchased by its self-chosen limitation of the scope of its enquiry. Science only considers impersonal experience, reality encountered as an object that we can manipulate and put to the experimental test. Its questions are framed in terms of efficient causes and not in terms of meaning or purpose. Its official discourse deals with measurements and not with values. As a methodological strategy, this narrow view has proved an effective technique for certain kinds of discovery. It would be a grave mistake—and one fatal for any serious quest for the basis of eschatological hope—to sup-

---

10. But, cf. J. C. Polkinghorne, *Beyond Science*, Cambridge University Press, 1996, ch. 8.

pose that the whole of reality can be caught in the wide meshes of the scientific net. To speak of music in terms of neural response to vibrations in the air is to say something of validity, but it falls far short of being able to embrace the mysterious reality of our experience when we listen to a Beethoven symphony.

An impersonal science, rightly evaluated as being no more than a component in the encounter with reality, provides no grounds for neglect of the significance of personhood. Nor do the insights of evolutionary biology into our kinship with other animals actually sustain the view, so often proclaimed by biologists, that there is nothing very special about being human. The fact is, we are self-conscious, God-conscious beings in a way that our animal cousins are not. We may share 99.5 percent of our DNA with chimpanzees, but that small difference is part of a very significant difference, just as the much smaller difference in DNA between myself and Mozart is part of a highly significant difference between an off-key whistler and a musical genius. The credibility of eschatological hope depends not only on belief in a faithful Creator but also on belief in the unique value of each human being. Right thinking eschatologically requires right thinking anthropologically.

The method of science is reductionist, to set to work to break down complexes into their more readily understood bits and pieces. We have seen that there are developments within the most modern science (pp. 16–17) that fight against this tendency and that encourage the consideration also of entities in their unreduced totalities. Yet, the overwhelming picture that the generality of science currently presents to us is of a reality to be comprehended in constituent terms. Religious insight and eschatological hope look in an entirely different direction, for the Source of their understanding lies in the transcendent dimension of total reality. Although the successes of the scientific reductionist approach carry no logical implication that this is the only path to truth, alogically it has had the effect of discouraging the pursuit of other ways of gaining knowledge.

It is not only a shallow scientistic triumphalism that has turned away from religious insight. Many people who can see that science of itself is too limited to tell us all that we need to know seem nevertheless to be at a loss to know where else to turn. In the face of this situation, religion must not lose its nerve in proclaiming that it too is concerned with the search for truth and understanding, albeit of a more profound and more elusive kind than that which is the focus of science.[11] Without recourse to the resources that theology can offer, we shall just be left either with the inadequacies of a purely physical eschatology or with vague longings and intuitions of hope whose substance and foundation are veiled from us.

Science lays great stress on the general and it discounts the particular. It is repeatable experience that can alone afford the basis for the experimental method. We must not allow ourselves to be bewitched by this methodological strategy. We know that all personal experiences, whether concerned with significant relationships, with encounter with beauty, with moral decision, with worship and discipleship, all have a unique and unrepeatable character. We never hear a Bach cantata the same way twice, even if we replay the same disc.

11. See J. C. Polkinghorne, *Belief in God in an Age of Science*, Yale University Press, 1998.

The unique value of individual experience forms part of the ground for the hope that that experience is not terminated by death. It is because Abraham, Isaac and Jacob are individually significant in their particularity that we believe that they matter to God and that they therefore have the hope of a destiny beyond their deaths (see Mark 12:24–27). The cultural recovery of the importance of the particular (sometimes called 'the deictic'[12]) is an essential prerequisite for a credible discussion of eschatology.

HOPE

Once again we return to the issue of hope. This human attitude is of religious significance because it points beyond the limits of the present and it must seek its ground beyond human individuals. Hope involves holding fast to promise in the context of apparent contradiction. The opposite of hope is despair, a nihilistic rejection of trust in the meaningfulness of life.

The contemporary cultural context that we have been discussing clouds recognition of the religious nature of hope, for it is prone to confuse it with optimism or with wishful thinking. Janet Soskice comments that even in the churches today there is a tendency to represent hope as if it were a psychological mood. 'Lack of faith and charity can be treated by prayer, but lack of hope is treated with antidepressants'.[13]

Because hope is much more than a mood, it involves a commitment to action. Its moral character implies that what we hope for should be what we are prepared to work for and

---

12. W. Stoeger, *Ends*, pp. 70–71.
13. J. M. Soskice, *Ends*, p. 78.

so bring about, as far as that power lies in us. As William Schweiker has pointed out, our moral life is conducted within a moral space, whose structure is characterised by the moral cosmology to which we subscribe.[14] By 'moral cosmology', Schweiker means a set of 'beliefs and valuations, often tacit in a culture, about how human beings orient themselves rightfully and meaningfully in the texture of the physical cosmos'.[15] In his estimation, there is a close association between moral cosmologies and conceptions of time. Schweiker understands the modern secular world to see time as 'empty', a void waiting to be filled by human choices and the meanings that we make for ourselves. The danger then is that unbridled moral autonomy leads to moral chaos. Opposed to this view is an apocalyptic moral cosmology, whose time is wholly filled with divinely imposed meaning. Schweiker fears that this leads to the danger of an external moral tyranny. Between these two extremes, he seeks to locate the moral cosmology of 'new creation' in which ' "new" is the transvaluation of our values, how we are enabled to respond to the goodness of existence and God's transformations of the patterns of life'.[16] This concept is largely 'realised' in its eschatological character and I shall later offer some theological considerations that point to the need for a strong futurist element also to be present in eschatological hope.

Hope based on an inaugurated eschatology is the foundation of a moral view that supports and enables the costly demands of fidelity and duty. A person's loyalty to an aging and debilitated parent or to a partner whose nature falls short of some notional ideal or to a handicapped child cannot be

14. Schweiker, *Ends*, ch. 9.
15. Ibid., p. 126.
16. Ibid., p. 137.

discharged without demands and restrictions being imposed upon the life of the one so committed. Hope can sustain the acceptance of such limitation by delivering us from the tyranny of the present, the feeling of need to grab as much as we can before all opportunity passes away for ever. We are enabled to live our lives not in the spirit of *carpe diem*, but *sub specie aeternitatis* (in the light of eternity). Hope enables the acceptance of existence and its possibilities and impossibilities as they actually are. In that acceptance, and not in some will-o'-the-wisp illusion of unrealistic and unattainable immediate perfection, lies the possibility of entering already into joy in this life. Realised eschatology finds its enabling in the hope sustained by a realistic futurist eschatology. What that future expectation might fittingly be is the subject we must next explore, making use first of the biblical tradition and then of Christian theological insight.

II

Biblical

Resources

CHAPTER FIVE

Old Testament Insights

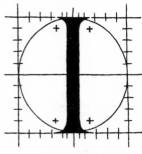F the crediblility of eschatological hope rests ultimately on the faithfulness of God, it is essential to seek knowledge of the divine nature as it has been made known through God's gracious acts of self-disclosure. For the Christian theologian, the Bible is not a convenient divinely dictated handbook in which to look up the answers, but it is the record of the persons and events that have been particularly open to the presence of divine reality and through which the divine nature may most transparently be discerned. Before we tackle theological reflection on the nature of future hope, we must survey the insights of eschatological relevance that are found in scripture.

Although the Hebrew Bible was written and compiled over a period between two and three thousand years ago, it continues to be relevant today not only because it records the history of Israel's encounter with God but also because its powerful imagery has inspired the writers of the New Testament and all subsequent generations of Christian thinkers. Eschatology is particularly dependent on the imaginative power of symbol for the framing of its discourse as it seeks to speak of 'what eye has not seen and ear has not heard' (1 Corinthians 2:9, loosely quoting from Isaiah 64 and 65). Refusal to make use of this resource would be a severe impoverishment. David Fergusson wrote that 'the preacher at Advent is charged not with discarding or demythologising the language of Scripture, so much as reappropriating its unique imaginative power'.[1]

Two aspects of the attitudes shown in relation to eschatological topics by the writers of the Hebrew Bible immediately strike the reader. One is their this-worldly preoccupation with the present life. The other is their conviction that Yahweh is the God who acts in history and does new things.

LIFE AND DEATH

Despite their closeness to a nation like Egypt that had so strong a concern with the after-life and an obsession with making detailed provision for it, the people of Israel centred their hopes on justice, prosperity and honoured old age, attained in the course of the life of this world. Hope for the future lay in the continuance of the nation and the family. The prophet's vision of fulfilment is when 'old men and old women shall again sit in the streets of Jerusalem, each with staff in their hand because of their great age' (Zechariah 4:5). When

1. D. Fergusson, Introduction, in D. Fergusson and M. Sarot (eds.), *The Future as God's Gift*, T & T Clark, 2000, p. 5. See also G. Green, ibid., ch. 4, for an extensive discussion of the role of imagination in eschatology.

Ezekiel has his great vision of the valley of dry bones that are revivified by the breath (*ruach*, spirit) of the Lord, it is the return of Israel from exile that he is prophesying, a redemption within history rather than a resurrection beyond history. 'I will put my spirit within you, and you shall live, and I will place you on your own soil' (Ezekiel 37:14).

Beyond death there is only the shadowy domain of Sheol, in which pale shades remain like fading carbon copies in a forgotten filing cabinet. There they are often thought of as being beyond the concern of Yahweh:

> Is your steadfast love declared in the grave,
> or your faithfulness in Abaddon?
> Are your wonders known in darkness,
> or your saving help in the land of forgetfulness?
> (Psalm 88:11-12)

Yet Psalm 139 depicts the dwellers in Sheol as being in the presence of the Lord (v. 8), and Job sees the post mortem life as being one of peaceful rest in which the inequalities of earthly life are obliterated (Job 3:13-19). Elsewhere in the book of Job, however, the picture is more sombre, with Sheol spoken of as 'the land of gloom and chaos, where light is like darkness' (Job 10:22). The existence of the shades is grey and subdued and it looks very unlike any dream of wish fulfilment. The God of Israel is the God of the living, an attitude that the wisdom writers endorse in their commonsense, matter-of-fact way. 'Whoever is joined with all the living has hope, for a live dog is better than a dead lion' (Ecclesiastes 9:4).

Nevertheless, Israel can certainly appeal to God for help in extreme trouble encountered in this life, experience symbolised as deliverance from the Pit, a desolate miry bog where the waters of chaos swirl around (Psalms 40:1–2; 64:1–3 and 15; and so on). Walter Brueggemann goes so far as to say,

> it is likely that it is unnecessary and unhelpful to distinguish the many rescues that occur in life with Yahweh and the "Big One" of life after death. All placements in the Pit are face to face with the power of death, and physical death is only an extreme case, different in degree but not in kind from all other threats to human life. It is characteristically enough in Israel to assert that "the Pit" is a reality, and that when Yahweh can be mobilised, the grip and threat of the Pit can be overcome.[2]

Be that as it may, it is certainly the case that only as the biblical period was coming to an end, do we find two verses in the Hebrew Bible that point clearly to a positive destiny beyond death: 'Your deeds shall live, their corpses shall rise. O dwellers in the dust, awake and sing for joy! For your dew is a radiant dew and the earth will give birth to those long dead' (Isaiah 26:19); 'Many of those who sleep in the dust of the earth shall awake, some to everlasting life, and some to shame and contempt' (Daniel 12:2). Both occur in passages that are concerned with the nation's struggle and suffering and which therefore wrestle with the perplexities arising from the fact that God's just judgement and deliverance do not seem to be being brought about within the course of present history. Although scholars think that the influence of Persian beliefs in an after-life played a part in this late Jewish concern with post mortem destiny, it is probable that the ambiguous fate of the martyrs in the Maccabean period also played an influential role. Could it be that Yahweh had finished dealings with those who had so bravely lost their lives as witnesses to the

2. W. Brueggemann, *Theology of the Old Testament*, Fortress, 1997, p. 554.

truth of the God of Israel? It is in the story from the inter-testamental literature of the woman who saw her seven sons tortured and killed before her eyes because of their adherence to the Law and their defiance of the tyrant Antiochus Epiphanes that we read the strongest Jewish affirmation that God's caring power extends beyond the grave. 'Therefore the Creator of the world, who shaped the beginning of humankind and devised the origin of all things, will in his mercy give life and breath back to you, since you now forget yourselves for the sake of his laws' (2 Maccabees 7:23).

The strongly platonic writer who composed the Wisdom of Solomon, affirms a belief in the God-given immortality of the human soul. After an account of the hopelessness of the ungodly, who can see nothing better than to indulge in a hedonistic life while there is still the opportunity to do so (Wisdom 2), we are told that 'the souls of the righteous are in the hand of God, and no torment will ever touch them . . . their hope is full of immortality' (Wisdom 3:1 and 4). This runs counter to the general Hebrew tendency to see human beings as animated bodies rather than incarnated souls.

In the period between the Old and New Testaments, a positive belief in a destiny beyond death began to grow among Jews. By the time of Jesus, there were many, including the Pharisees, who held the hope of a resurrection on the Last Day, though the conservative Sadducees continued to deny such a belief (see Acts 23:8).

GOD IN HISTORY

The strong reserve of the writers of the Hebrew Bible itself about what might lie beyond history contrasts strikingly with

Israel's confidence in her God as the God who acts within history. This confidence did not arise from some facile optimism but it was forged in the fire of disaster and disappointment. In the tradition there was recorded not only the great deliverance from slavery that took place in the Exodus from Egypt but also the destruction of the Temple and the deportation that took place in the Exile into Babylon. This latter event is the nadir of Judah's historical fortune. Walter Brueggemann follows Walter Zimmerli in calling it the *nullpunct* (point zero). However, he also sees it as the mysterious moment in which something new is brought to birth, expressing 'the wounded but undefeated, affronted but not alienated, shamed but not negated resolve of Yahweh to have a people—this people, this same people, this deported people—as Yahweh's own people in the world'.[3] Brueggemann compares this Jewish experience of hope in adversity, of promise held onto at the centre of contradiction, to the Christian experience of Easter.

Meanwhile we may note that the psalms of lament express in more personal terms a similar conviction of God's faithfulness. Starting with frankly expressed complaint at the experience of apparent abandonment, they end with praising the Lord for the divine continuing care. 'How long, O Lord? Will you forget me for ever? How long will you hide your face from me? . . . But I trusted in your steadfast love; my heart shall rejoice in your salvation' (Psalm 13:1 and 5).

It is certainly the prophets associated with the events of the Exile who most clearly speak of God's ability to spring surprises in history by bringing into being what is wholly new. Second Isaiah is emphatic that God is not tied to the

3. W. Brueggemann, *Ends*, p. 146.

repetition of past deeds. 'See the former things have come to pass, and new things I now declare; before they spring forth, I tell you of them'. (Isaiah 42:9). 'I am about to do a new thing; now it springs forth, do you not perceive it. I will make a way in the wilderness, rivers in the desert'. (Isaiah 43:19). Ezekiel gives an immensely detailed description of the New Temple (Ezekiel 40-44), that will replace the one destroyed by Nebuchadnezzar's armies. Jeremiah looks forward to God's new covenant with Israel (Jeremiah 31:31-34) in which the divine law will be written within, upon the human heart (cf. Ezekiel 36:26-27). The Hebrew word for new (*chadash*) is not particularly common in the Bible, but a significant proportion of its occurrences are found in these three prophets.[4]

Of course, the new that God brings about is envisaged by these prophets as lying within the future unfolding of present history. It is in Third Isaiah, the prophet of the return from exile (an experience which did not correspond to the anticipated restoration or enhancement of former glories), that we find the clear proclamation of the hope of a yet more radical novelty: 'For I am about to create a new heavens and a new earth; the former things shall not be remembered or come to mind. . . . The wolf and the lamb shall feed together, the lion shall eat straw like the ox; but the serpent—its food shall be dust! They shall not hurt or destroy in all my holy mountain, says the Lord' (Isaiah 65:17 and 25, the latter echoing the earlier Isaiah 11:6-9). Here we may discern the seed of what was to grow into the Christian conviction of God's intention to bring into being a 'new creation'.

---

4. R. Bauckham and T. Hart, *Hope Against Hope*, Darton, Longman and Todd, 1999, p. 78.

More sombre, but also lying within the future discerned by the prophets, is 'the Day of the Lord', a day of both vindication and judgement for all the nations. Israel is not to presume upon what she may think to expect from that fateful occasion. 'Is not the day of the Lord darkness and not light?' (Amos 5: 20; see also Isaiah 2:12; Joel 2:1–2; Malachi 3:2; and so on). Later, Christian thinking would derive from this tradition the sequence *Dies irae, dies illa,* sung in the Mass for the dead in the liturgy of the medieval Western Church.

APOCALYPTIC

A yet more radical attitude to the future is expressed in that type of writing that is called apocalyptic, which many believe developed out of the prophetic tradition. As the name suggests, an apocalypse is an 'unveiling' of heavenly secrets, either about the nature of the heavenly realm itself, or about the course and end of history. The second half of the book of Daniel (7–12) is the most striking Old Testament writing of this latter kind. It is characteristic of apocalyptic that it emerges at times of trial and persecution (Daniel was written during the persecution of faithful Jews by the Seleucid king, Antiochus Epiphanes) and that it envisages God's bringing about a cataclysmic time of radical change in which the present age is transmuted into the new age, in which evil is totally defeated and God's reign is absolutely and visibly established. The time of this transition is frequently presented as being preceded by a period of great and unparalleled woe: 'There shall be a time of anguish, such as never occurred since nations first came into existence' (Daniel 12:1).

Most apocalyptic writing is pseudonymous, being attributed to a powerful figure of the past, such as Daniel at the court of King Nebuchadnezzar. If the writing takes the form of an historical survey, this allows the actual writer to incorporate known events in his past into the story, before adding speculations about the future. Thus elements of continuity and discontinuity are present even in apocalyptic, but the final denouement is so drastic that the motif of discontinuity dominates. It seems as if the pessimism generated by severe persecution can be assuaged only by the crudest and most overwhelming images of the destruction of the enemy.

Apocalyptic writings proliferated in the intertestamental period. In the New Testament there is the little apocalypse of the synoptic gospels (Mark 13:5–27, par.) and, of course, Revelation. It is interesting that the latter is not pseudonymous, for its origin is clearly attributed to the visionary experiences of John of Patmos (Revelation 1:9).

FURTHER ESCHATOLOGICAL THEMES

A number of other themes occur in the Old Testament which the Christian Church was to find to be a fruitful source for its own eschatological reflections. The verse most frequently quoted in the New Testament is Psalm 110, v. 1: 'The Lord says to my Lord, "Sit at my right hand until I make your enemies your footstool" '. No doubt this was originally an expression of confidence that the Lord would grant the king victory over his earthly enemies but, interpreted as a symbol of the heavenly session at the right hand of God, the verse helped the early church to consider how the Lordship of Christ related to the fundamental Lordship of the one God of Israel. Yet the authority thus bestowed still remained implicit and veiled.

'As it is, we do not yet see everything in subjection to him' (Hebrews 2:8). Therefore one might expect a future event in which what is now hidden will be made manifest in the final appearing (*parousia*) of our Lord Jesus Christ (cf. Acts 3:20–21). The understanding of the Second Coming as the symbol of the final vindication of the Lordship of Christ (cf. 1 Corinthians 15:28) is one that is still accessible to us today.

An insistent theme throughout the Old Testament is that of the blessing and cursing that flow from God's judgements within history upon the obedient and the disobedient. 'See, I am setting before you today a blessing and a curse' (Deuteronomy 11:26). Patrick Miller emphasises that the divine purpose is in the blessing and not in the curse.[5] In the promise to Abraham, the ones who will find in him a blessing are plural, while the one who does not is singular. 'I will bless those who bless you and the one who curses you I will curse; and in you all the families of the earth shall be blessed' (Genesis 2:3). In Miller's view, 'critical to a proper understanding of judgement is an awareness of its ultimately *redemptive* purpose'.[6]

This hopeful theme is reinforced by the image of the Messianic Banquet. 'On this mountain, the Lord of hosts will make for all peoples a feast of rich food, a feast of well-matured wines, of rich food filled with marrow, of well-matured wines strained clear' (Isaiah 25:6). The Christian will think of Jesus' many meals at which sinners and outcasts were welcome, of the parable of the wedding feast (Matthew 22:1–10, par.), of the Last Supper, and of the continuing celebration of the Eucharist throughout the centuries. We are even told

5. P. Miller, *Ends*, p. 165.
6. Ibid., p. 161.

that at this great feast God will 'swallow up death for ever' (Isaiah 25:8).

The concept of the Messiah ('the anointed one') is one that in Christian thinking came to carry strong eschatological meaning as its fulfilment in the risen Lord Jesus, (whose title 'Christ' is the Greek equivalent of Messiah) was understood and explored. In the Old Testament, it is the king who is the Lord's anointed, and messianic hopes, usually expressed using other metaphors such as 'the Branch', are of a Davidic deliverer, whose acts in history will restore the glories of the former kingdom (for example, Isaiah 9:6-7; 11:1-5, though see also the following verses, 6-9, for symbolic indications of more radical expectations; Zechariah 3:8-10, but see also 4:11-13, where two anointed ones are mentioned).

Life is seen in the Hebrew Bible as God's gift, rather than as a purely natural phenomenon. It is the Lord who breathes into Adam the breath of life after he has been formed from the dust of the ground (Genesis 2:7). It is the Spirit of God that is the source of all life:

> When you hide your face, they are dismayed;
> when you take away their breath, they die and return
>   to their dust.
> When you send forth your spirit, they are created;
> and you renew the face of the ground.
>   (Psalm 104:29-30)

Two other concepts from the Old Testament are used by the New Testament writers with eschatological significance. One is the figure of the Son of man, drawn from the great vision of Daniel 7, where he appears before the Ancient of Days as the books are being opened in judgement. All four gospels place the phrase 'the Son of man' on the lips of Jesus and (with the trivial exception of John 12:34) on the lips of no other. The only other places in the New Testament where the phrase is used are by Stephen when he sees a heavenly vision (Acts 7:56) and twice in Revelation (1:17; 14:14). In the latter case, the phrase appears in the Greek without the article that is usually present in the gospels. (It is difficult to evaluate the significance of this difference, since in what one may assume to be the underlying Aramaic there could not be an article.) New Testament scholars have argued interminably about what to make of all this. In semitic languages, the phrase 'son of man' is a perfectly natural way of referring to a human being, in contrast to the oddness of the phrase in both Greek and English. Certainly the phrase in the gospels sometimes looks as though it amounts to no more than an oblique manner of self-reference, rather like the English use of 'one'. Yet at other times (for example, Matthew 10:23; 12:40; 13:41; 16:27-28; 19: 28; 24:27, 30, 37, 39, 44; 26:24) the reference is clearly specific and eschatological. Is this latter usage, so reminiscent of Daniel 7, a retrojection by the early church or a remembrance of a mode of self-identification used by Jesus himself? I personally believe that the phrase goes back to Jesus, as he drew on the Hebrew scriptures for an understanding of his vocation.[7] Its eschatological overtones would, in that case, be of considerable significance, as is perhaps also the apparent mixture of individual and corporate character that the phrase seems to carry in Daniel, where the Son of man is not only a striking single figure, but he is also correlated in some way with the community of 'the holy ones of the Most High' (Daniel 7:18).

7. See C. F. D. Moule, *The Origins of Christianity*, Cambridge University Press, 1977, pp 11-22; J. C. Polkinghorne, *Science and Christian Belief/The Faith of a Physicist*, SPCK/Princeton University Press, 1994, pp. 98-100.

Finally we should take note of the institution of the Sabbath. Its eschatological significance has been an important theme in the writings of Jürgen Moltmann. He sees sabbath rest as breaking the relentless flow of present time, imposing a rhythmic return upon its linearity, recalling the divine rest after the acts of creation (Genesis 2:1-3), and pointing towards the endless Sabbath (sometimes called 'the eighth day'), which will be creation's consummation. 'Every sabbath celebration is a messianic intermezzo in time, and when the messiah comes, he will bring the final messianic sabbath for all God's created beings'.[8] Moltmann links the Sabbath with the Shekinah, the indwelling glory of God's presence in the midst of God's people. The word itself does not appear in the Hebrew Bible, but the reality to which it refers is symbolised in the pillar of fire of the Exodus wanderings and in the cloud of glory that is said to have filled Solomon's temple at the time of its dedication (1 Kings 8:10-11; see also Exodus 40:34-5; Ezekiel 10:15-22). Moltmann sees the Sabbath as the symbol of the redemption of time and the Shekinah as the symbol of the redemption of space.[9]

We can conclude our survey of Old Testament material by returning to Second Isaiah who, speaking in the name of the Lord, proclaims to an exiled Israel, 'Do not fear' (Isaiah 41:10 and 14). Walter Brueggemann comments, 'The antidote seems modest in the the face of the threat. Unless the antidote is uttered by one who is trustworthy. Everything depends upon that'.[10] The ultimate eschatological issue, and the only adequate ground of hope, is the everlasting faithfulness of God.

8. J. Moltmann, *The Coming of God*, SCM Press, 1996, p. 138.
9. Ibid., pp 279-308.
10. Brueggemann, *Ends*, p. 154.

CHAPTER SIX

The Resurrection of Jesus

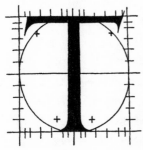HE New Testament is written in the light of its authors' conviction that God raised Jesus Christ from the dead. Without the recognition of that belief, much of its discourse is not fully intelligible. It is necessary, therefore, to begin an engagement with the New Testament material by addressing the question of whether such a belief in the resurrection is still credible today, at the start of the twenty-first century.[1]

THE RIDDLE OF JESUS

When we compare Jesus of Nazareth with other great religious figures, such as Moses, the Buddha or Mohammed, some obvious similarities are present. All are wise speakers whose words convey powerful insight; all have a charismatic ability

1. See J. C. Polkinghorne, *Science and Christian Belief/The Faith of a Physicist*, SPCK/Princeton University Press, 1994, ch. 6

to influence other people; all are credited with remarkable deeds. Yet, there is one big difference between Jesus and the rest. They end their lives in honoured old age, surrounded by disciples who are resolved to continue the work and message of the Master. Jesus, on the other hand, dies in midlife, shamefully and painfully executed, undergoing a form of death that pious Jews regarded as a sign of God's rejection ('anyone hung on a tree is under God's curse'; Deuteronomy 21:23). Indeed he himself cries out in the the darkness of his dying, 'My God, my God, why have you forsaken me?' (Matthew 27:46; Mark 15:34). His followers have all run away, except for a small band of faithful women who weep at the foot of the cross. Peter will angrily deny that he ever knew Jesus, an embarrassing anecdote that all four gospels faithfully record. It seems a story of absolute failure—at best, a good man eventually beaten by the system; at worst, a deluded man whose pretensions fell away in the face of stark reality. I believe that if this sorry sight were the actual end of the story of Jesus, we would never have heard of him. He would simply have disappeared from historic recollection, as presumably has often happened to apparently charismatic figures who prove to fall short of their claimed expectations. Yet we have all heard of Jesus, and that in itself is a significant fact about him. The riddle of Jesus is why someone whose life seemed to end in complete failure has proved to be the most influential figure in the history of the world.

Within just a few weeks of his miserable death, those same frightened followers are again in Jerusalem, but now facing up to the authorities who earlier had seemed so daunting, and proclaiming that this Jesus, this rejected and crucified man, has been made by God 'both Lord and Messiah' (Acts 2:36). That is to say, they believe that uniquely in him

God's will and salvific purpose are being fulfilled. Our task is to understand how this tremendous change came about. Such a remarkable transformation requires a commensurately remarkable cause. The first disciples claimed that it was because 'God raised him up, having freed him from death, because it was impossible for him to be held by its power' (Acts 2:24). Who Jesus was, and what his real significance was, turns on whether this claim is true. The resurrection is pivotal for Christian belief.

APPEARANCES

The earliest Christian appeal to evidence that Jesus was raised from the dead is found in Paul's first letter to the Corinthians, written about 55. (The crucifixion itself was either 30 or 33.) In this writing, which antedates Mark, the first gospel to be written, by at least ten years, Paul says,

> I handed on to you as of first importance what I in turn had received: that Christ died for our sins in accordance with the scriptures, and that he was buried, and that he was raised on the third day in accordance with the scriptures, and that he appeared to Cephas, then to the twelve. Then he appeared to more than five hundred brothers and sisters at one time, most of whom are still alive, though some have died. Then he appeared to James, then to all the apostles. Last of all, as to someone untimely born, he appeared also to me. (1 Corinthians 15, 3–8)

When Paul refers to what he himself 'received', it is natural to interpret this as referring to the instruction he would have been given following his dramatic conversion on the road to Damascus. This would link the material of 1 Corinthians to a time only two or three years after the events to which it

refers. The antiquity of this highly condensed summary is supported by its use of the Aramaic *Cephas* to refer to Peter, and
the phrase 'the twelve' to refer to the apostles, both of which
are usages that very soon lapsed in the early church. Therefore, this testimony takes us very close to its subject matter.
It is clearly intended to have evidential value, hence the reference to witnesses 'most of whom are still alive'. Yet its spare
list of those who had seen the risen Lord does not make it at
all clear what this experience might have been like. For further information on that, one must turn to the later accounts
given in the gospels.

A bewildering scene awaits us. All four gospels tell essentially the same story of the events leading up to the crucifixion.
Of course, there are minor differences, notably in relation to
exactly what Jewish and Roman judicial processes were fol-
lowed, but there can be no real doubt, in this case, about the
general compatibility of the sequence of events presented by
the evangelists. When it comes to the aftermath of the death
of Jesus, however, there are strange deviations between the accounts that are given of the appearances.

Mark's gospel, at least in the form that we have preserved
for us in the authentic manuscript tradition, does not contain an account of a resurrection appearance at all, though one
in Galilee is clearly foretold (Mark 14:28; 16:7). The story
concludes on a note of silent fear (Mark 16:8). (The verses
that follow in many English translations are later additions.)
Donald Juel has explored the starkness of this strange ending.
His words are sometimes bleak. 'And when the women run
away, too terrified to tell anyone what they have seen, we are
left without the means of ending the story. There is no one
to trust or doubt, no one whose word can be tested. There is

only the fearful silence'.[2] Of course, Juel acknowledges that elsewhere the New Testament has much more to say about resurrection. But he goes on to comment: 'That Jesus was raised from the dead may be as unsettling as the reality of his death. For some, it will be the most unsettling of all.'[3] Not all our contemporaries will welcome the 'something more' that resurrection represents. 'How to speak of resurrection requires artfulness. The mark of theological wisdom is to know when and how to speak of such matters in a way that avoids an escape from the reality of death—and that prevents closing off the future to new possibilities for those who take strange solace in the finality of death'.[4]

The other gospels present a clearer and more positive picture. Matthew's main appearance story is located in Galilee, with a minor story of an appearance to the women in Jerusalem. The latter combines elements of both joy and fear (Matthew 28:8-10). For Luke, everything happens in Jerusalem on the first Easter day itself, including the appearance to the two on the road to Emmaus. John has accounts both of appearances to the disciples in Jerusalem and also of a lakeside appearance by the Sea of Galilee. There is no obvious reconciliation in detail between these stories and the list given by Paul.

Such perplexing diversity might at first seem to be indicative of a gaggle of made up stories, with each writer following his fancy in the version that he gives. I am persuaded, however, that this is not the case. Despite the variety of circumstances and detail, there is a surprising common thread

2. D. Juel, *Ends*, p. 178.
3. Ibid., p. 181.
4. Ibid.

in these gospel accounts. This thread is that it was difficult to recognise the risen Christ. Many of the stories centre on a moment of recognition and disclosure. Mary Magdalene initially mistakes Jesus for the gardener, only realising who he is when he speaks her name (John 20:14-16). Only the beloved disciple has the insight to recognise the figure standing on the lakeshore in the light of early dawn (John 21:4-7). The couple on the road to Emmaus realise who it is with whom they have been talking only at the very end of their journey, and then he vanishes from their sight (Luke 24:30-31). Most strikingly of all, in Matthew when Jesus appears on the Galilean hillside, though many fall at his feet to worship him, we are also told with considerable frankness that 'some doubted' (Matthew 28:17). They were unable to attain that moment of recognition. Such a non-triumphalist indication of the problematic character of recognising the risen Christ, so variously expressed, seems to me much more likely to be the kernel of an historical reminiscence than a feature curiously common to a bunch of made up tales.

In considering the variety of the appearance stories, and also their comparative lack of detail about the content of conversations with the risen Christ, we need to bear in mind that there would have been something intimate in these encounters which did not necessarily lend itself to full public disclosure. There are clear hints of an individual appearance to Peter (Luke 24:34; 1 Corinthians 15:5), but no story of this meeting of Jesus with the one who had so vehemently denied him. Perhaps that had to remain private to Peter. (The communal encounter in Galilee [John 21:1-19], in which Peter participated in a special way, has overtones of reconciliation, but it does not seem to me that it can be that individual appearance obliquely referred to elsewhere.)

Outside the gospels, there is the story of Christ's appearance to Paul on the Damascus road, three times retailed in Acts (9:3–9; 22:6–11; 26:12–18), and also testified to by Paul himself (1 Corinthians 9:1; 15:8; Galatians 1:11–16). This story seems at first sight different from the others not only because it occurs so much later but also because of its character, centring on the shining of a light from heaven. Nevertheless, it is Jesus who speaks to Paul out of the heavenly brilliance. Some have wondered whether the vision in the Revelation of John of the One who is alive for evermore, and who holds the keys of Death and of Death's Domain (Revelation 1:12–18), is also an account of a resurrection appearance. However, the New Testament seems quite capable of discriminating between visionary experience, however impressive (for example, Acts 18:9–10; 23:11; 2 Corinthians 12:3–5), and those fundamental encounters with the risen Christ that are the ground of Apostleship.

The experiences of the witnesses to the resurrection have both an objective and a subjective dimension to them. On the one hand, the stories not only contain moments of recognition but also, in a way that modern sensibility often finds disturbing,[5] they involve palpability (Matthew 28:9; Luke 24:39; John 20:24–27) and even the eating of food (Luke 24:41–43). On the other hand, there are the subjective elements of the light experiences and of hearts strangely warmed. In the subjective dimension there is some kinship with standard

5. Critics often reject these stories as legends, apparently simply on the grounds of their uncongeniality to modern thought that prefers a more 'spiritual' way of thinking.

grief processes in the bereaved, in which it is quite common for people to believe that they see or hear the loved one who has died, but the appearance stories, in their intensive life-enhancing character, go beyond these fleeting experiences.[6]

The character of the appearance narratives definitely excludes a mere notion of resuscitation, as if Jesus had simply returned for a further spell of ordinary life. Michael Welker drily observes that 'nowhere does the Bible have a person say "Good that you are back again, Jesus!" '[7] The risen Christ is transformed. He appears and disappears at will and he is able to enter locked rooms. His presence is the manifestation of a glorified life that transcends the everyday existence of this present world. Yet his body still bears the marks of the passion. Writing about the unique character of the resurrection appearances, Welker says,

> It is important that the biblical texts do not try to smooth over the problems connected with this presence. They describe the fear, the doubt, the division, and the disbelief connected with this reality. . . . On the whole, the resurrection witnesses very calmly acknowledge that this presence is not a simple empirical reality, although it bears several characteristics of such a reality. On the one hand, the experiences of the resurrected Christ and of his reality are as varied and unique as our own individual experiences of love, joy, trust and sorrow are various, highly unique, never fully communicable, and certainly not experimentally reproducible. On the other hand, according to the witnesses of the scriptures, the experiences of the resurrected Christ are quite the opposite of any existential expressions that either are beyond words or can only be narrated individually. All the witnesses to the resurrected

6. See F. Watts, *Ends*, pp. 54-55.
7. M. Welker, *Ends*, p. 283.

Christ refer to the new presence, the presence in a different mode of the pre-Easter Jesus.[8]

THE EMPTY TOMB

A second line of testimony relating to the resurrection of Jesus
is found in the stories of the discovery of the empty tomb.
All four gospels give accounts of this incident, differing in details such as the exact time of day and the precise number and
names of the women, but clearly in essence as much at one
with each other in this respect as they are in their accounts
of the last days of Jesus' earthly life. Yet many critics have
looked askance at the empty tomb tradition. They ask, if it
is so significant, why does not Paul make any overt reference
to it? Of course, an argument from silence derived from such
occasional writings as the Pauline letters, is a pretty weak one.
Also one may ask why, in that extremely condensed account
of 1 Corinthians 15:3–8, does Paul take the trouble to say that
Jesus 'was buried', unless he knew that there was indeed a tomb
and that this was a matter of some importance. It is hard to
believe that a first-century Jew like Paul, conceiving of human
beings as psychosomatic unities, could have held the conviction, that he unquestionably did, that Jesus was alive and yet
also believed that his body still lay mouldering in a grave.

It was certainly generally the case that the Romans cast
the bodies of executed felons into a common grave, but we
know from archaeological evidence that this was not an in-
variable practice. The story of Joseph of Arimathea begging
the body of Jesus from Pilate is not an impossible one, and it
is hard to see, were it just a made-up tale, why the otherwise

8. Ibid., p. 284.

obscure Joseph was assigned to this honourable role—unless, of course, he actually fulfilled it. Even more improbable in a concocted story, would be making women its principal protagonists. Their depressed status in the ancient world did not permit them to be treated as valid witnesses. (That, perhaps, is why they are not mentioned by Paul in 1 Corinthians 15.) Much the most likely reason for their appearing in this role is that they were actually present and made their startling discovery.

It is also important to recognise that whatever problems modern scholars may have felt about the empty tomb tradition, it was not a difficulty that was shared by either the opponents or proponents of Christianity in the ancient world. In the controversies between Jews and Christians (an argument that we can trace back into the first century; see Matthew 27: 62–66; 28:11–15), it is common to both sides that there was a tomb and that it was empty. Where the disagreement lay was in what had brought this about, the critics of Christianity claiming that it was because the disciples had stolen the body in an act of deliberate deceit, a suggestion that is surely incredible in view of their subsequent staunch commitment, even to the point of martyrdom. Even less persuasive are the suggestions, arising much later in the continuing debate, that Jesus was not really dead when taken down from the cross and that somehow he revived in the tomb and made his way out of it (as if so debilitated a figure could have persuaded the disciples that he was victor over death), or that there was a mistake about the identity of the tomb, so that Christianity arose from an error that no one bothered to look into and put right.

We have seen that, in the gospels, in contrast to a certain kind of modern apologetic, the empty tomb is initially a disturbing and problematic discovery. It induces fear and perplexity in those who make it (Matthew 28:5; Mark 16:8; Luke 24:4-5; John 20:2). It requires explanation. In the tradition, angelic messengers have to make it clear what is its significance, for no one was expecting a resurrection within history, but only at the last day (see John 11:24). It seems to me that, despite its somewhat late appearance in the recorded tradition, the story of the empty tomb is to be taken with the greatest seriousness, with its implication that the glorified body of the risen Christ is the transmuted form of his dead body. The theological significance of this is a matter to which we shall return later.

PAULINE REFLECTION

The same fifteenth chapter of 1 Corinthians, in which Paul gives us the earliest account of testimonies to the resurrection, is also the one in which he gives the most extended reflection to be found in the New Testament on what is the significance of this great event.

Paul agrees with the assessment we have already made that here is the pivot on which Christian belief turns. 'If Christ has not been raised, then our proclamation has been in vain and your faith has been in vain' (v. 14). He sees the resurrection as an event of universal significance, the foretaste and guarantee enacted within history, of a destiny that awaits all of us beyond history. 'As all die in Adam, so all will be made alive in Christ' (v. 23).

This leads Paul to consider what is the relationship between the life of this world and the resurrected life of the world to come. 'Someone will ask "How are the dead raised? In what body do they come?"' (v. 35). It is interesting to note that in attempting to answer he has recourse to the *science* of his day, using the analogy of the seed that 'dies' in the ground before it can grow into something different in the form of the plant that sprouts from it. Paul appeals to the different kinds of flesh found in different living animals, and to the difference that it was then supposed existed between the terrestrial and the celestial realms. Paul knows that true eschatological hope must lie in a radical transformation brought about by God's act of resurrection, and not in the mere prospect of a resuscitation. He is certain that 'flesh and blood cannot inherit the kingdom of God, nor does the perishable inherit the imperishable' (v. 50; see also, vv. 42–44).

Paul got engaged, just as the participants in the eschatological research project at Princeton got engaged, in wrestling with the eschatological necessity to hold in balance both continuity and discontinuity, if a credible hope is to be articulated. There must be enough continuity for persons to have their individual destinies beyond death. It is not enough for there simply to be new people with the old names. Yet there must also be sufficient discontinuity to deliver us from the non-hope of the eternal return of this world of transience.

Paul speaks of our present life as involving a *soma psychikon*, while the life of the world to come will involve a *soma pneumatikon* (v. 44). These Greek phrases are notoriously difficult to translate into English. The New Revised Standard Version's 'physical body' and 'spiritual body' do not succeed in catching all the nuances. An essential point is that both are *bodies*, a word no doubt to be understood in the Hebrew sense of a complete animated being. In that case, *soma pneumatikon* is not be thought of as some ethereal entity, the oxymoron of a body made of spirit, but rather as a being totally suffused by the life-giving spirit of God. We shall have to return later to considering this issue from a more contemporary perspective, as we continue to wrestle with the theme of continuity/discontinuity that already so perplexed Paul in the middle of the first century.

In fact, we may detect some degree of development in Paul's own thinking in the course of his apostleship. His earliest letter, 1 Thessalonians, presents a distinctly more sharp and dramatic picture of eschatological consummation, expressed through the descent of the Lord from heaven and the rapture of believers to meet him in the air (1 Thessalonians 4:16–17), than does the corresponding picture in 1 Corinthians (1 Corinthians. 15, 51–7), though the same trust and hope in the risen Christ undergirds both mythological images. (Much eschatological truth must be expressed in mythic terms, since ultimate reality lies beyond the scope of a prosaic vocabulary based on experience of this present world.) One influence on Paul's developing thinking may have been the growing recognition that the end of history was not going to follow almost immediately after Christ's resurrection.

CONTEMPORARY CONSONANCE

The New Testament has supreme importance for the Christian as the record of the foundational experiences of the first Christian community in its encounter with its risen Lord. Although those initiating experiences are unrepeatable, so that the apostolic witness to the resurrection must have a unique significance, yet, if we are to be able to enter into that heritage for ourselves, there must be a deep resonance between what was experienced then and what is our experience today. Canonic memory must be able to link the past with the present in a warm and living relationship. In fact, the confession of the Christian Church down the centuries has always been 'Jesus lives!' Its discourse of Christ has not been in terms of a respectful recollection of a founder figure, but in the joyful acknowledgement of the living Lordship of Christ in the present.

For most Christians, the focus of this experience will lie in the sacrament of the Eucharist. The celebrating priest often begins the great prayer of thanksgiving, that lies at the heart of the liturgy, with the proclamation 'The Lord is here!' Christians have differed in their understandings of how Christ is present in the sacramental action, but testimony to his real presence is a vital part of the Christian worshipping experience.[9] Christian faith centres on the living Christ who is 'the same yesterday, today and for ever' (Hebrews 13:8).

Michael Welker has particularly emphasised the continuing role of the community of witnesses, testifying in each generation to the reality of their living Lord. 'The memory that Jesus established in the celebration of the Lord's Supper allows the canonic memory — on the basis of the biblical traditions — to become highly concentrated, concrete and existential. . . . It is through the working of God's creativity that the memory of Christ does not sink to a merely historical process, or even to a multitude of remembrances'.[10] The power of this testimony is such that Welker can say, 'The knowledge of Jesus' resurrection is just as little an illusion as the discovery of justice or of mathematics'.[11]

9. See M. Welker, *What Happens in Holy Communion?* Eerdmans, 2000, ch. 5.
10. M. Welker, *Ends*, p. 287.
11. Ibid., p. 283.

CHAPTER SEVEN

Further New Testament Insights

THE KINGDOM OF GOD

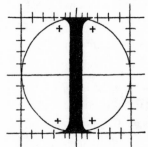 N Mark's gospel, Jesus begins his public ministry with the declaration, 'The time is fulfilled, and the kingdom of God has come near; repent and believe the good news' (Mark 1:15). One thing about which virtually all scholars can agree is that the proclamation of the kingdom of God—that is, of God's rule over all God's people—was a central part of Jesus' teaching. Christoph Schwöbel writes that 'the imminent coming of the kingdom of God is a center of Jesus' message, and when he is confessed as the Messiah, the Son of the living God, the coming of the kingdom of God is so closely related to his person that he is in his person seen as the coming of the kingdom of God'.[1] A d v e n t

Much disagreement remains, however, about the nature of Jesus' expectation of the kingdom, correlating with the

1. C. Schwöbel, *Ends*, p. 111.

theological disagreements that exist about how to envisage eschatological fulfilment. If one takes an apocalyptic view of the latter, the anticipation would be that the kingdom would irrupt suddenly into the present order of the world, constituting an abrupt divine act of radical transformation. Johannes Weiss and Albert Schweitzer believed that this was the form of Jesus' expectation and that he deliberately sought his own immolation in an attempt to force God's hand in the matter. C. H. Dodd, on the contrary, developed the point of view of a realised eschatology, which sees the kingdom as being already present in words and deeds of Jesus' ministry. Others again, including the present writer, adopt the familiar eschatological stance of already/not yet, believing that it is necessary to combine elements of both realised and futurist eschatology, in what one may call an inaugurated, but not completed, eschatology. *proleptic*

The gospels certainly seem to give support to this last view. Jesus speaks of the presence of the kingdom, particularly in relation to those exorcisms in which the demonic opponents of the kingdom are cast out (Mark 12:28 par.). In reply to an enquiry from some Pharisees about when the kingdom is coming, he says: 'The kingdom is not coming with things that can be observed; nor will they say, "Lord, here it is!" or "There it is!" For in fact the kingdom of God is among you' (Luke 17: 20–21). Or, perhaps, 'the kingdom of God is within you', for the way in which the verse should be translated is unclear. Yet Jesus also tells us to pray: 'Your kingdom come' (Matthew 6: 10 par.). In the 'little apocalypse' (Mark 13:5–27 par.), there is an account of the last stages of history in which a prophecy of the destruction of Jerusalem (which actually took place in 70) and a description of the end of the world, are interwoven in a stark and challenging way, though the kingdom itself is not mentioned.

Much of Jesus' teaching about the kingdom is in the form of parables. Some of these are parables of growth (the mustard seed; leaven; the patient farmer; wheat and tares). Hans Weder sees in these parables of growth a recognition of the creativity active within creation that can encourage the hope of a continuance beyond the necessary end of that creation.[2]

LIFE AFTER DEATH

The issue of that continuance to which Weder refers is addressed by Jesus, in the case of human life, in the course of an encounter with the Sadducees (Mark 12:18-27 par.). Religiously conservative, these influential Jewish leaders accepted the authority of only the first five 'books of Moses', that make up the *Torah* in the Hebrew Bible. They did not feel that they found in it any statement that there is a human destiny beyond death, and so this was not part of their belief. They put their sceptical point of view to Jesus in the form of a dilemma arising from an ingeniously concocted story in which a woman is successively the wife of seven brothers, each of whom dies without issue, thereby imposing on the next the duty of marrying his widow. If there were to be a life to come, how could the complicated tangle of this-worldly relationships be resolved? 'In the resurrection, whose wife will she be?' (v. 23). Jesus, in a characteristic manner, cut through this ingenious speculative smokescreen to get to the heart of the matter. He took the Sadducees back to Exodus, a book whose authority they

2. H. Weder, *Ends*, pp. 196-202.

acknowledged, in which God speaks to Moses at the burning bush, saying 'I am the God of Abraham, the God of Isaac and the God of Jacob'. Jesus then comments, 'He is the God not of the dead, but of the living; you are quite wrong' (v. 27).

The argument is powerful indeed. If the patriarchs mattered to God once—and they certainly did—they must matter to the faithful God for ever. They will not simply be discarded at their deaths. This is one of the most important New Testament passages relating to human destiny post mortem. It points to the everlasting faithfulness of God—the divine steadfast love—as the only, and the totally sufficient, ground for the hope that our lives will not end at death.

So far, we have concentrated on the synoptic gospels. In John, the phrase 'the kingdom of God' only occurs twice (John 3;3 and 5), though Jesus speaks of his own kingdom, which is 'not of this world', when he is before Pilate (John 18:36). Elsewhere in the fourth gospel, it is the phrase 'eternal life' that plays a rather similar role to that of the kingdom of God in the synoptics. John has a quite strongly realised emphasis in his speaking of the present experience of eternal life (for example, John 4:14; 5:24; 7:37-8; 17:2-3; but see John 5:28-9).

The rest of the New Testament testifies to the belief that in the risen Christ the believer has been given a new and enduring life. 'Therefore we have been buried with him by baptism, so that, just as Christ was raised from the dead by the glory of the Father, so we too might walk in newness of life. For if we have been united with him in a death like his, we will certainly be united with him in a resurrection like his' (Romans 6:4-5). Once again, it is trust in the faithfulness of God that is the ground of this hope. 'For this reason it depends on faith, in order that the promise may rest on grace and be guaranteed to all [Abraham's] descendents ... in the presence of the God in whom he believed, who gives life to the dead and calls into existence things that do not exist'. (Romans 4:16-17). It is the Spirit already at work within us who is the testimony to life beyond the grave. 'If the Spirit of him who raised Jesus from the dead dwells in you, he who raised Jesus from the dead will give life to your mortal bodies also through his Spirit who dwells in you' (Romans 8:11). Schwöbel comments that 'it is the Spirit of God who bridges the eschatological tension between the now already and not yet'.[3]

NEW CREATION

In 2 Corinthians, Paul uses the concept of the new creation as a way of expressing the Christian eschatological hope. 'If anyone is in Christ, there is a new creation: everything old has passed away; see everything has become new!' (2 Corinthians 5:17). There is a clear resonance with the expectation, found in the exilic prophets, of the acts of the God who is not bound to the past, but who has future surprises in store. From the perspective of the New Testament, however, the reference is not solely to the future. The new creation is 'in Christ' and it is his resurrection that is the seed from which the new has already begun to grow.

The scope of this new creation is cosmic and it is not limited to human destiny alone. In one of the most remarkable passages in the whole of the New Testament, Paul speaks of a universal hope:

3. Schwöbel, *Ends*, p. 119.

> For the creation waits with eager longing for the revealing of the children of God; for the creation was subjected to futility, not of its own will but by the will of the one who subjected it, in hope that the creation itself will be set free from its bondage to decay and will obtain the freedom of the glory of the children of God. We know that the whole creation has been groaning in labour pains until now; and not only the creation, but we ourselves, who have the first fruits of the Spirit, groan inwardly while we await for adoption, the redemption of our bodies. (Romans 8:19-23)

We may link these words with the figure of the Cosmic Christ presented to us in the first chapter of Colossians, by whom 'all things in heaven and on earth were created' and in whom 'all things hold together' (Colossians 1:16-17). We are told that 'through him God was pleased to reconcile to himself all things' [not just all people], whether on earth or in heaven, by making peace through the blood of his cross (Colossians 1:20).

The vision of a world transformed is also set forth in the great symbol of the new Jerusalem, with which the book of Revelation draws to its close:

> Then I saw a new heaven and a new earth; for the first heaven and the first earth had passed away, and the sea was no more. And I saw the holy city, the new Jerusalem, coming down out of heaven from God, prepared as a bride adorned for her husband. And I heard a loud voice from the throne saying, See, the home of God is among mortals. He will dwell with them; they will be his peoples, and God himself will be with them; he will wipe every tear from their eyes. Death will be no more; mourning and crying and pain will be no more, for the first things have passed away. (Revelation 21:1-4)

Elsewhere, that strange book gives us chilling pictures of the sufferings at the end of time and of a divine judgement in which those whose names are not written in the book of life are cast into the lake of fire and undergo the second death. These violent images have about them something of the crudity and vividness of an animated cartoon. Yet they are punctuated by powerful representations of the eternal worship of heaven (Revelation 4; 5:8-14; and so on).

Another writer also called John gives us an altogether different concept of judgement. The fourth evangelist sees it as self-imposed, resulting from a failure to recognise and respond to divine reality. 'And this is the judgement, that light has come into the world, and people loved darkness rather than light because their deeds were evil' (John 3:19).

The chaotic flurry of symbols that makes up Revelation contains another image that has exercised the Christian speculative imagination, probably to an undue extent. This is the millenary expectation of the thousand year rule of the saints, ending in the final release of Satan and the subsequent defeat of him and his henchmen (Revelation 20:4-10). Jürgen Moltmann has given a careful and extensive discussion of the history and varieties of millenarian thought, emphasising that its original concern was with hope for the martyrs, whose unconditional decision for truth against falsehood seemed to require a particular vindication.[4] Millenarian expectation interleaves present history with future eschatological hope, in a way that parallels Moltmann's own thinking. He believes that the thousand year rule of Christ and the saints will be a neces-

---

4. J. Moltmann, *Theology of Hope*, SCM Press, 1967, pp. 261-65; *The Coming of God*, SCM Press, 1996, pp. 146-202.

sary bridge passage between the old and new creations. This belief leads him to assert that 'Christian eschatology—eschatology, that is, which is messianic, healing and saving—is millenarian eschatology'.[5] Many of us remain unconvinced of the need for such a transitional episode. *purgatory*

Yet another symbol of the end that has exercised the Christian imagination, often in unedifying ways, has been the final resurgence of evil through the appearance of the Antichrist (2 Thessalonians 2:3-12; 1 John 2:18-23; Revelation 13: 5-18; 17:3-8; 19:19-21). Believers have often been all too ready to apply the title to those from whom they differed. Whatever may be the ultimate significance of the symbol, it certainly serves to remind us—were a reminder necessary after the history of the twentieth century—of the continuing and mysterious force of evil active within the old creation. Colin Gunton has said that for the Christian there is no 'cheap hope'[6] for true fulfilment lies the other side of suffering and death. We should also remember that the New Testament portrays the Antichrist as appearing with all the trappings of a false religion.

HOPE REVISITED

Hans Weder points out that the new Testament is concerned with a process that he calls 'the purification of hope'.[7] A meretricious desire for marvels (Herod's disappointed hope of seeing Jesus perform a miracle; Luke 23:8), or a longing for

5. Moltmann, *Coming of God*, p. 202.

6. C. Gunton, 'Dogmatic Theses on Eschatology', in D. Fergusson and M. Sarot (eds.), *The Future as God's Gift*, T & T Clark, 2000, p. 140.

7. H. Weder, *Ends*, pp. 185-88.

purely political deliverance (the redemption of Israel; Luke 24:21), have to be changed into the true hope that arises from the death and resurrection of Christ. Earthly expectations miss the point, for they neglect the significance of the unseen realities on which true hope actually rests. 'For in hope we were saved. Now hope that is seen is not hope. For who hopes for what is seen? But if we hope for what we do not see, we wait for it with patience' (Romans 8:24-25). Hope and faith inextricably intertwine, since the One who is trustworthy is the ground of hopeful expectation. Therefore we may add to those passages to which Weder refers, the testimony of the Writer to the Hebrews, who tells us that 'faith is the assurance of things hoped for, the conviction of things not seen' (Hebrews 11:1). After accounts of some heroes of faith, we are told that 'they desire a better country, that is a heavenly one. Therefore God is not ashamed to be called their God; indeed he has prepared a city for them' (Hebrews 11:15-16).

The theme of hope also intertwines with that of the delay of the final fulfilment of God's purposes. A late writing in the New Testament canon portrays the scoffers as saying: 'Where is the promise of his coming? For ever since our ancestors died, all things continue as they were from the beginning of creation' (2 Peter 2:4). The writer's response is that 'the Lord is not slow about his promise, as some think of slowness, but is patient with you, not wanting any to perish, but all to come to repentance' (2 Peter 3:9). From our twenty-first century vantage point that enables us to survey the fifteen-billion-year evolutionary history of the universe, it is even easier for us to understand that the Creator is patient and subtle, one who is very far from being a God in a hurry. In his study of an approach to theology through music, Jeremy Begbie draws an analogy with the role of delay in a musical composition. 'Through its layered patterns of tension and resolution, music relies for much of its effect on generating a sense of the incompleteness of the present, that not all is now given. Theologically, the dynamic of promise and fulfilment is an obvious correlate of that'.[8] Already/not yet is an intrinsically necessary component of our eschatological thinking.

The theme of delay is also linked with that of the veiled mystery concerning the timing of God's eschatological action. 'But of that day or hour no one knows, neither angels in heaven, nor the Son, but only the Father' (Mark 13:32 par). Over Christian history, too much ill-judged speculation has attempted to penetrate that veil. The true response of hope is an alert expectancy, summed up in the repeated New Testament injunction to keep awake and be on the watch (Mark 13:33–37; Romans 13:11; and so on). We encounter here the theme of Christ's Second Coming (the Parousia). The New Testament does not only see Jesus as the One who has come but as the One who is to come. The Church must continue to pray *maranatha* (Come Lord!; see 1 Corinthians 16:22b; Revelation 22:20). Gerhard Sauter comments that 'the title of Coming One for Jesus Christ is not an appendix to Christology that can be surgically removed if it starts to cause discomfort. Rather the title forms Christology as a whole'.[9]

As we move towards the theological discussion of eschatological hope, one of our central concerns will be to see the

---

8. J. Begbie, *Theology, Music and Time*, Cambridge University Press, 2000, p. 99. Chapter 4 of this book is concerned with eschatological issues.

9. G. Sauter, *What Dare We Hope?* Trinity Press International, 1999, p. 50.

extent to which these insights, so powerfully expressed in the pages of scripture, can be made our own today, in a world whose cosmology and self-understanding are in so many ways very different from that of the centuries in which the biblical material was compiled.

III

Theological

Approaches

CHAPTER EIGHT

The God of Hope

THEOLOGICAL HOPE

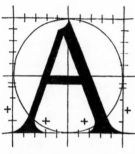s we begin our consideration of the theological approach to eschatological issues, we need to return yet again to the question of hope. This theological virtue is a matter of central concern for a credible articulation of Christian belief, which must seek a total understanding of God and God's purposes, capable of embracing not only the possibilities of the present but also the sufferings of the past and the expectations of the future. Jürgen Moltmann said that 'From first to last, and not merely in the epilogue, Christianity is eschatology, is hope, forward looking and forward moving, and therefore also revolutionary and transforming the present'.[1] Fifty years earlier, Karl Barth had said more or less the same: 'Christianity that is not entirely and altogether eschatology has entirely and altogether nothing to do with Christ'.[2]

1. J. Moltmann, *Theology of Hope*, SCM Press, 1967, p. 16.
2. K. Barth, *The Epistle to the Romans*, Oxford University Press, 1933, p. 314.

Hope is the negation both of Promethean presumption, which supposes that fulfilment is always potentially there, ready for human grasping, and also of despair, which supposes that there will never be fulfilment, but only a succession of broken dreams. Hope is quite distinct also from a utopian myth of progress, which privileges the future over the past, seeing the ills and frustrations of earlier generations as being no more than necessary stepping stones to better things in prospect.

If eschatology is to make sense, all the generations of history must attain their ultimate and individual meaning. Christianity takes the reality of evil seriously, with all the perplexities that entails. It 'refuses the premature consolation that pre-empts grief, the facile optimism which cannot recognise evil for what it is'.[3] As part of its unflinching engagement with reality, Christianity will recognise the seriousness of science's prediction of ultimate cosmic futility (ch. 1). As part of its unflinching engagement with history, Christianity will recognise that episodes like the Holocaust deny to it any shallow conception of what hope for the future might mean, as if it could be divorced from acknowledgement of the horror of the past.

Holding in mind such a clear-eyed view of the woes and disappointments of history, one must ask what could then be the ground of a true hope beyond history? There is only one possible source: the eternal faithfulness of the God who is the Creator and Redeemer of history. Here Christianity relies heavily upon its Jewish roots. It is only God who can bring new life and raise the dead, whose Spirit breathes life into dry

3. R. Bauckham and T. Hart, *Hope Against Hope*, Darton, Longman and Todd, 1999, p. 42.

bones and makes them live (Ezekiel 37:9–10). Hope lies in the divine *chesed*, God's steadfast love, and not in some Hellenistic belief in an unchanging realm of ideas or an intrinsic immortality of the human soul. Christian trust in divine faithfulness is reinforced by the knowledge that God is the One who raised Jesus from the dead. Only such a God could be the ground for that hope against hope that transcends the limits of any natural expectation.

This means that a credible eschatology must find its basis in a 'thick' and developed theology. A kind of minimalist account of deity, which sees God as not much more than the Mind behind cosmic order, will not be adequate. Nor will a kind of minimalist Christology, which sees Jesus as no more than an inspired teacher, pointing humanity to new possibilities for self-realisation and with his message living on in the minds of his followers, provide a sufficient insight into the divine purposes for creation beyond its death to be the ground of an everlasting hope. These concepts are too weak to bear so great a weight of expectation. To sustain true hope it must be possible to speak of a God who is powerful and active, not simply holding creation in being but also interacting with its history, the one who 'gives life to the dead and calls into existence the things that do not exist' (Romans 4:17). This same God must be the one whose loving concern for individual creatures is such that the divine power will be brought into play to bring about these creatures' everlasting good. The God and Father of our Lord Jesus Christ is just such a God.

To be persuasive, eschatological hope requires more than a general intuition that something must survive death. The problems that beset the realistic hope of a post mortem destiny are complex and demanding. They call for a corresponding richness and depth in our understanding of the power and steadfast love of God.

The question of eschatological hope is also the question of the fundamental meaningfulness of human life within creation. Are those moments of our deep experience when we glimpse that reality is trustworthy and that all will be well, intimations of our ultimate destiny or merely fleeting and illusory consolations in a world of actual and absolute transience? Moltmann says,

> Our question about life, consequently, is not whether our existence might possibly be immortal, and if so what part of it; the question is: *will love endure,* the love out of which we receive ourselves, and which makes us living when we ourselves offer it.[4]

If God is, as Christians believe, the God of love, then love will indeed endure. 'Many waters cannot quench love, neither can floods drown it' (Song of Solomon 8:7) — not even the waters of cosmic chaos nor the tumultuous breakers of human evil.

FORGIVENESS AND JOY

Hope, then, must involve the redemption of the past as well as a promised fulfilment in the future. Indeed, the one requires the other. If it is to be true and total, hope must look in both directions. One may ask where participation in such an all-embracing hope could find its setting in human life. Two important sources are our experiences of forgiveness and of joy, the one freeing us from the tyranny of the past, the other offering us a foretaste of the ultimate future.

4. J. Moltmann, *The Coming of God*, SCM Press, 1996, p. 53; my italics.

Without forgiveness there can be no redemption of the past. God's forgiveness comes to us through the cross of Christ, 'the lamb of God who takes away the sin of the world' (John 1:29). This forgiveness frees us from the shackles with which we have enslaved ourselves. Equally necessary for our liberation is the forgiveness that we give to others for the hurts that they have inflicted on us. Resentment and the desire to pay back are distorting and corrupting influences from which we must seek to be released. In the New Testament, the receiving and giving of forgiveness are often seen as parts of a single action, linked together because they are mutually necessary (the Lord's prayer: Matthew 6:12; 6:14-15; 18:35; and so on).

It is a costly business to forgive a real wrong, and a costly business also to receive forgiveness for a real wrong committed. Such actions centre on the recognition of a painful reality. They are far removed from the trivial indifference of 'It doesn't matter'. The drunken motorist actually killed the innocent child and he has to acknowledge that this is so. In an act of astonishing generosity, the bereaved parent can nevertheless rise above the natural desire to seek punitive revenge. The grace of God is powerfully at work in such a situation. Acts of forgiveness offer experience of a ground of hope for the redemption and healing of the past. Christoph Schwöbel writes, 'Every experience of gratuitous forgiveness offers vindication of eschatological hope'.[5]

Our experiences of joy, those deep moments of peaceful happiness that come to us through music, art, nature and human love, and through the worship of God, are foretastes of

---

5. C. Schwöbel, *Ends*, p. 122.

the fruits of eschatological fulfilment (cf. 2 Corinthians 1:22). These are insights of a dynamic and unifying kind. Miroslav Volf says that 'Joy lives from *the movement in time* qualified by an unperturbed peace between past and future in all presents'.[6] A vision of what that might ultimately mean is beautifully expressed in a prayer based on some words of John Donne:

> Bring us, O Lord, at our last awakening into the house and gate of heav'n, to enter into that gate and dwell in that house, where there shall be no darkness nor dazzling, but one equal light; no noise nor silence, but one equal music; no fears nor hopes, but one equal possession; no ends nor beginnings, but one equal eternity; in the habitation of thy glory and dominion, world without end.

REALISED ESCHATOLOGY

But is it necessary for there to be a 'last awakening' for this kind of experience to be consummated? In *The End of the World and the Ends of God*, Kathryn Tanner presented a powerful account of a realised eschatology of the present moment, whose ultimate quality lies precisely in its character of being this life lived in relationship with God. In her 'thought experiment' she argued for an *eschatologia continua*, paralleling the widely accepted concept of *creatio continua* in which God's unfolding creative purposes are being fulfilled within the evolutionary processes of the universe. Just as the emphasis of the doctrine of creation properly lies in God's upholding of the world in being at every moment and not in the instant of its beginning, so Tanner believes that the emphasis of eschatology should lie

6. M. Volf, *Ends*, p. 275.

in the attainment of a life lived with God now and not in some future state of blessedness beyond death. 'Old and new are found together in the world we know'.[7] She comments that 'so understood, eternal life presents a more spatialised than temporalised eschatology'.[8] It is life lived at the present moment in the presence of God. Such ideas have been popular with many theologians, from Friedrich Schleiermacher to Paul Tillich.

Yet, while an emphasis of this kind offers a healthy corrective to a purely futuristic, 'pie in the sky' kind of eschatology, it seems by itself to be an inadequate expression of the Christian hope. This life is too hurtful and incomplete to be the whole story. What are we to make of those whose lives are tragically cut short, or grievously oppressed and distorted by their circumstances? They too must have their share in the kingdom of God. Tanner is strong in making a call for action to right the wrongs of this world: 'complacency is ruled out not by a transcendent future but by a transcendent present— by the present life in God as the source of the goods that the world one lives in fails to match'.[9] But such action can, at best, be only half the story. Without a transcendent future, many are condemned to a loss of good that no process solely within history could ever restore to them. In fact, all of us are so condemned, even if we have the good fortune to die in honoured and pious old age. We shall all die with unfinished business and incompleteness in our lives. There must be more to hope for.

Similar difficulties attend the concept of an atemporal 'objective immortality' that simply sees each human life as being preserved in its totality in the eternal memory of God,

7. K. Tanner, *Ends*, p. 236.
8. Ibid., p. 230.
9. Ibid., p. 234.

an idea that has been popular with process theologians and with some other thinkers.[10] Either such lives are preserved as much with their sins as with their good deeds, as much with their frustrations as with their achievements, or they are held in a purged and purified form that would be a false memory of the one to whom it purports to relate. Actual eschatological fulfilment demands for each of us a completion that can be attained only if we have a continuing and developing personal relationship with God post mortem. We must participate in our own salvation. As Miroslav Volf says, speaking of God's ultimate act in the redemptive justification of the sinner, 'In soteriology, the "objects" of justification are always persons, never their done deeds or lived lives'.[11] The basic issue here is whether temporality is constitutive of being truly human, an essential good and not an unfortunate deficiency. This is a point to which we shall return.

THE SACRAMENTAL LIFE

It is in the sacramental life that there is for the Christian a balanced expression of the roles of past, present and future. Schwöbel says that 'like all acts of the church the sacraments are characterised by the twofold reference back to Christ and forward to the kingdom of God'.[12] In many modern liturgies, the worshippers exclaim in the course of the great prayer of thanksgiving, their threefold belief that 'Christ has died, Christ is risen. Christ will come again'. Past, present and future are held together in the sacramental moment. It is within

10. See J. Hick. *Death and Eternal Life*, Collins, 1976, pp. 104–9; M. Volf, *Ends*, pp. 259–70.
11. Volf, *Ends*, p. 263.
12. Schwöbel, *Ends*, p. 118.

the tradition of the Orthodox that the eschatological character of the Eucharist has been most clearly preserved, as they
understand the earthly congregation to be participating in the
everlasting worship of heaven. The bread and wine that are
elements of this creation are also the body and blood of Christ,
elements of the new creation.

Paul reminded the Romans of something that he pre-
sumes every Christian believer to know, that baptism is also
an eschatological act in which we die to the world and live to
Christ. 'Do you not know that all of us who have been baptised in Christ Jesus were baptised into his death? Therefore
we have been buried with him by baptism into death, so that,
just as Christ was raised from the dead by the glory of the
Father, so we too might walk in newness of life' (Romans 6:3–
4). Yet Paul also says that 'If for this life only we have hoped in
Christ, we are of all people most to be pitied' (1 Corinthians
15:19). The name that we are given at baptism must endure.
The eternal life that begins here must continue, through the
faithfulness of God, in a destiny beyond our deaths. Concerning that eternal life, Michael Welker writes that,

> It is the fullness of the life of Christ that can rightly be
> called "eternal life". This life in its worth and glory does
> not depend upon memory. It is no less fulfilled under the
> cross than in Christ's parousia. In this life the witnesses
> gain a share and give a share. By this life they are enobled
> and made holy. Participation in this life is the ground of
> Christian hope.[13]

God is the God of hope because God is the God of past,
present and future. The risen Christ is the one who is 'the first

13. M. Welker, *Ends*, p. 288.

and the last, and the living one. I was dead, and see, I am alive
for ever, and I have the keys of Death and Death's Domain'
(Revelation 1:17–18). Those who embrace hope place themselves in the hands of the Lord of the open future. To do so is
an act of total commitment to the One who is faithful. In the
words of Gerhard Sauter, 'This is when eschatology finds its
proper subject: the perception of the living God who by his
promises discloses a way that we can go without being clear
about where it may lead us and without being given any means
to measure distances'.[14] There is an apocryphal saying attributed to Martin Luther, in which he declared that if he knew
that tomorrow the world would end, he would plant an apple
tree today. Eschatological hope is that nothing of good will
ever be lost in the Lord. That thought in itself is enough to
rebut a kind of other worldly piety that neglects the ethical
demands of the present. It assures us that our strivings for the
attainment of good within the course of present history are
never wasted but will bear everlasting fruit.

14. G. Sauter, *Ends*, p. 213.

CHAPTER NINE

Personhood and the Soul

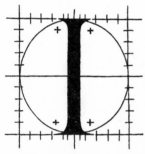 F human beings have a destiny be-
yond death that is much more than
a mere resuscitation (which would
amount to no more than another turn
of the wheel of this transient world),
then what is it that will connect our
present life to our future life in that
new world whose character will be so different? We face here,
in a critical way, the issue of continuity and discontinuity that
lies at the heart of all attempts to gain a degree of eschatological understanding. What could it be that ensures that it
is indeed Abraham, Isaac and Jacob who live in the kingdom
of God, and not just new beings who have been given the
old names?

THE SOUL

In the course of Christian thinking, an answer to these questions has frequently been made by appeal to the concept of the

soul, conceived of in a platonic fashion as a spiritual entity, released from imprisonment in the fleshly body at the moment of death. While there are still body/soul dualists of this kind,[1] for many people this has become an extremely problematic way of conceiving of human nature. Our evolutionary history appears to link us in a continuous way with our primate ancestry, which in turn can be traced back through simpler life forms to the bacteria who, for two billion years, were the sole living inhabitants of Earth. Although it cannot absolutely be ruled out that at some stage, the Creator adjoined a separate and additional spiritual component to complement evolving bodies of increasing complexity, once those bodies had reached the appropriate stage of development, the idea seems contrived and unpersuasive to many. They find greater theological satisfaction in the concept of the divine sustaining of a process of continuous creation through evolutionary development.

The striking effects that physical incidents, such as brain damage or drug intake, can have on human personality also encourage taking a psychosomatic view of the nature of human beings. A celebrated case, often referred to in this connection, is that of Phineas Gage. In 1848, this efficient and capable construction foreman was involved in a terrible accident in which a premature explosion drove an iron bar through the front of his brain and out of the top of his head. Astonishingly, he survived and within two months was declared physically healed. However, his personality was completely changed. Gage had become fitful and capricious, endlessly restive and quite in-

1. J. C. Eccles, *The Human Mystery*, Springer, 1979; R. Swinburne, *The Evolution of the Soul*, Oxford University Press, 1986.

capable of holding down a job. It was clear that the gross damage to the brain that he had sustained had completely changed the character and equilibrium of his mind. We may conclude, from this and much other evidence, that human beings look much more like animated bodies than like incarnated souls.

Despite both Hebrew thought and much of the thinking of the New Testament being in accord with this unitary view of human nature, a difficulty might be feared to ensue for the coherence of eschatological hope. We must ask whether, in consequence of this anti-dualist conclusion, one has lost the possibility of speaking of the human soul altogether, so that there is no longer a way in which we may frame an understanding of a destiny beyond death, expressed in terms of the soul's provision of the necessary element of continuity required to make such a belief meaningful. I do not think that this is the case.[2]

Whatever the human soul may be, it is surely what expresses and carries the continuity of living personhood. We already face within this life the problem of what that entity might be. The soul must be the 'real me' that links the boy of childhood to the ageing academic of later life. If that carrier of continuity is not a separate spiritual component, what else could it be? It is certainly not merely material. The atoms that make up our bodies are continuously being replaced in the course of wear and tear, eating and drinking. We have very few atoms in our bodies today that were there even two years ago. What does appear to be the carrier of continuity is the immensely complex 'information-bearing pattern' in which

2. J. C. Polkinghorne, *Science and Christian Belief/The Faith of a Physicist*, SPCK/Princeton University Press, 1994, p. 163.

that matter is organised. This pattern is not static; it is modified as we acquire new experiences, insights and memories, in accordance with the dynamic of our living history. It is this information-bearing pattern that is the soul.[3]

We have already seen (chapter 2) how modern science, through its study of complex systems, is beginning to recognise the importance of information as a complement to energy in the description of the process of the world. The concept of the soul that has just been proposed is fully in accord with this development. I believe that we can follow Thomas Aquinas in adopting, in appropriately modern phrasing and understanding, the concept of the soul as the form, or information-bearing pattern, of the body. Of course, our present understanding of these profound matters is not sufficient for us to be able to frame an adequate account of what such a conception could mean in detail, but there does seem to be the prospect of a coherent, if inevitably somewhat conjectural, way of holding together human psychosomatic unity with human personal identity. It would be altogether too crude to say that the soul is the software running on the hardware of the body—for we have good reason to believe that human beings are very much more than 'computers made of meat'[4]—but that unsatisfactory image catches a little of what is being proposed.

3. The point of view presented here corresponds to a form of dual aspect monism (see J. C. Polkinghorne, *Faith, Science and Understanding*, SPCK/Yale University Press, 2000, ch. 5.4). It bears some relationship to the non-reductive physicalism of W. Brown, N. Murphy and H. N. Malony (eds.), *Whatever Happened to the Human Soul?* Fortress, 1999. However, I prefer the more evenly balanced dual-aspect terminology, and I do not set store by supervenience as an explanatory category.

4. R. Penrose, *The Emperor's New Mind*, Oxford University Press, 1989, ch. 10; J. Searle, *Minds, Brains and Science*, BBC Publications, 1984.

While the soul, understood in this way, has a dynamic and changing character, it is perfectly possible to suppose that, amid its evolving change, each individual soul carries specific elements of its patterning which are the signature of its own abiding and unique personal identity. (A mathematician would say that there were invariant characters, preserved in the course of unfolding transformation.)

Finally, we may note that it would even be possible to reconcile this concept of the soul with a highly modified form of platonism. We have spoken earlier of an everlasting realm of mathematical entities (p. 20). It would be conceivable that the information-bearing patterns of the soul could be considered as intersecting with this realm and that they would remain lodged there after the decay of the body. However, for the reasons already given, I prefer a thorough-going psychosomatic picture of human nature, in which the preservation of the soul depends only on divine faithfulness. Of course, the resurrection re-embodiment of the soul would in any case have to be God's act.

DESTINY BEYOND DEATH

If these ideas contain some truth, we have to acknowledge that this information-bearing pattern will, in the course of nature, be dissolved by the decay of our bodies after death. There is, therefore, no intrinsic immortality associated with the soul in this way of understanding it. Death is a real end. However, it need not be an ultimate end, for in Christian understanding only God is ultimate. It is a perfectly coherent hope that the pattern that is a human being could be held in the divine memory after that person's death. Such a disembodied existence,

107

Life is changed but not ended

even if located within the divine remembrance, would be less than fully human. It would be more like the Hebrew concept of shades in Sheol, though now a Sheol from which the Lord was not absent but, quite to the contrary, God was sustaining it. It is a further coherent hope, and one for which the resurrection of Jesus Christ provides the foretaste and guarantee, that God in the eschatological future will re-embody this multitude of preserved information-bearing patterns in some new environment of God's choosing. (What that environment might be we shall discuss in the chapter that follows.)

In other words, there is indeed the Christian hope of a destiny beyond death, but it resides not in the presumed immortality of a spiritual soul, but in the divinely guaranteed eschatological sequence of death and resurrection. Only a hope conceived of in this way can do full justice to human psychosomatic unity, and hence to the indispensibility of some form of re-embodiment for a truly human future existence. The only ground for this hope—and the sufficient ground for this hope, as we have already emphasised—lies in the faithfulness of the Creator, in the unrelenting divine love for all creatures.

Some philosophers have objected to the idea of re-embodiment without intervening physical continuity, on the grounds that if it were possible, then what would prevent the multiplication of replicas, with the incoherence of personal identity that would result. The answer is surely that only God has the power to effect such re-embodiment and divine consistency would never permit the duplication of a person.

A number of further comments need to be made. As expressed so far, the emphasis placed on information-bearing pattern has had a strongly individualistic tone. However, we must recognise that the deep relationality of creation (chapter 2), and the significant distinction between a human person (constituted in relationships) and a mere individual (treated as if existing in self-isolation), encourage a broader view. The 'pattern that is me' cannot adequately be expressed without its having a collective dimension. In this connection, it is significant that a powerful way of articulating Christian eschatological destiny is through the incorporation of believers into the one 'body of Christ' (1 Corinthians 12:27; Ephesians 4:12–13). It is also important to recognise, as Miroslav Volf emphasises, that eschatological fulfilment must involve the mutual reconciliation of human beings. 'Persons cannot be healed without the healing of their specific socially constructed and temporarily (*sic*) constructed identities'.[5]

In the following chapter we shall consider temporal aspects of how this present world and the new world of the resurrected life to be may be related to each other. A more immediate, intimate and pastorally sensitive issue is how we are to conceive of the relationship between the living and the dead. Moltmann presses upon us the importance of addressing the question, 'Where are the dead?'[6] Earlier, he had written that 'the idea of an enduring communion between the living and the dead in Christ, and of the community of Christ as a communion of the living and the dead is a good and necessary one'.[7] Moltmann recalls that in the base communities of South America, when the roll is called of the names of those who 'dis-

5. M. Volf, *Ends*, p. 262.
6. J. Moltmann, *Ends*, pp 246–47.
7. J. Moltmann, *The Coming of God*, SCM Press, 1996, p. 98.

appeared' in the troubles, the congregation all say 'Presente'. He comments that 'the community of the living and the dead is the praxis of resurrection hope'.[8]

If the souls awaiting the final resurrection are held in the mind of God, as we have suggested, then 'in the Lord' there will surely be a mediated relationship between the living and the dead. One of the most natural ways in which to express this relationship will be through prayer. No doubt, those who are 'in Christ' are wholly within God's loving care and protection, but we should not argue that this makes it unnecessary or inappropriate for us to pray for them. After all, the same is as true of those among the living who are committed to Christ, as it is of the departed. Many arguments alleged against praying for the dead seem, on the face of it, to apply equally to praying for the living. Of course, we must rid our prayers for the dead of some unfortunate and unedifying medieval distortions. We are not involved in an instrumental manipulation on their behalf, as an unreformed notion of 'masses for the dead' might have seemed to suggest. Prayer is always mutual participation in grace and never the exercise of a quasi-magical power. It is significant that the Eastern Orthodox Christians, always so sensitive to eschatological reality, hold intercessions for the dead but offer no masses on their behalf.

In the patristic period there was some speculation about what age people will be at the resurrection. A popular answer was about thirty, not only because it could be seen as corresponding to some climactic in human life but also because it was believed to be the age at which Jesus died and rose

8. Ibid., p. 108.

again. In terms of our present discussion, this ancient argument could be rephrased by asking at what state of its dynamic development will the information-bearing pattern of the human person be reinstantiated in the re-embodied resurrection life. As with many other detailed eschatological questionings, one might be tempted to reply, 'Wait and see'. Yet a very serious concern lies behind the query, not least in relation to those who through enduring dementia and the ravages of Alzheimer's disease have suffered a kind of partial death within the confines of this life. A similar issue relates to those who through severe congenital disability may be thought, in some ways at least, only to have attained to a limited kind of life in this world. We might ask, also, in what condition will Phineas Gage be resurrected?

We do not need to suppose that being held in the mind of God is a purely passive kind of preservation. We may expect that God's love will be at work, through the respectful but powerful operation of divine grace, purifying and transforming the souls awaiting resurrection in ways that respect their integrity. Ultimately, what has been lost will be restored and what of good was never gained will be bestowed. In chapter 11 we shall consider the divine eschatological process of redemptive fulfilment, but we do not need to suppose that this is wholly confined to the resurrected life of the new creation. It may begin in whatever post mortem state precedes that final destiny, a thought that the New Testament language of 'Paradise' (Luke 23: 43) and being 'with Christ' (Philippians 1: 23) may be held to encourage. Yet its ultimate fulfilment must wait upon the restoration of complete embodied human personality. The workings of divine grace will not only involve the healing of disability and the restoration of decay, but it may also be expected to begin its work within all of us, for we shall all need God's sanctifying and redeeming touch beyond what we have already experienced in this world.

CHAPTER TEN

The New Creation

COSMIC HOPE

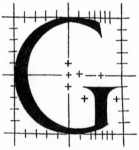 OD must surely care for all creatures in ways that accord with their natures. Therefore, we must expect that there will be a destiny for the whole universe beyond its death, just as there will be a post mortem destiny for humankind. We have seen that two remarkable New Testament passages (Romans 8:18-25; Colossians 1:15-20) do indeed speak of a cosmic redemption. Just as we see Jesus' resurrection as the origin and guarantee of human hope, so we can also see it as the origin and guarantee of a universal hope. The significance of the empty tomb is that the Lord's risen and glorified body is the transmuted form of his dead body. Thus matter itself participates in the resurrection transformation, enjoying thereby the foretaste of its own redemption from decay. The resurrection of Jesus is the seminal event from which the whole of God's new creation has already begun to grow.

The risen Christ is no resuscitated corpse. His body has new properties that enable it, at his will, to appear and disappear within present history. Nor will the redeemed universe be a mere repetition of its present state. This current universe is a creation endowed with just those physical properties that have enabled it to 'make itself' in the course of its evolving history. A world of this kind, by its necessary nature, must be a world of transience in which death is the cost of new life. In theological terms, this world is a creation that is sustained by its Creator, and which has been endowed with a divinely purposed fruitfulness, but which is also allowed to be at some distance from the veiled presence of the One who holds it in being and interacts in hidden ways with its history. Its unfolding process develops within the 'space' that God has given it, within which it is allowed to be itself. This is a theme that has been developed particularly by Jürgen Moltmann.[1] He draws on the Kabbalistic notion of *zimzum*, the divine making way for the existence of created reality. One may sum up this insight by saying that this creation is the result of a kenotic act by the Creator, who has made way for the existence of the created other.[2] The physical fabric of such a universe must take a particular form, but there is no reason to suppose that the Creator cannot bring into being a new creation of a different character when it is appropriate to the divine purpose to do so.

The world to come will indeed have to have a different character. Just as Jesus was exalted to the right hand of the Father after his resurrection, so the world to come will be integrated in a new and intimate way with the divine life. I do

1. See J. Moltmann, *The Trinity and the Kingdom of God*, SCM Press, 1981, pp. 105-13; *God in Creation*, SCM Press, 1985, ch. 4.
2. See J. C. Polkinghorne (ed.), *The Work of Love*, SPCK/Eerdmans, 2001.

not accept panentheism (the idea that the creation is in God, though God exceeds creation)[3] as a theological reality for the present world, but I do believe in it as the form of eschatological destiny for the world to come. As Paul wrote to the Corinthians, God will then be 'all in all' (1 Corinthians 15:28). The Eastern Orthodox speak of eschatological fulfilment as being the attainment of *theosis*, not meaning by that that creatures will become gods but that they will share fully in the divine life and energies. This world is one that contains the focussed and covenanted occasions of divine presence that we call sacraments. The new creation will be wholly sacramental, suffused with the presence of the life of God. In his great vision of the End, the seer of Patmos saw the holy city as one in which there was no longer a cultic temple 'for its temple is the Lord God the Almighty and the Lamb' (Revelation 21:22). God's presence, veiled from us today, will be open and manifest in the world to come. Moltmann has his own way of expressing this hope, in terms of the descent of the divine Shekinah.

These are great hopes, in which the necessarily discontinuous side of eschatological expectation finds its expression. Much has to be taken on trust, for it is clearly beyond our feeble powers to conceive exactly how a redeemed universe will function. Yet it seems a coherent hope to believe that the laws of its nature will be perfectly adapted to the everlasting life of that world where 'Death will be no more; mourning and crying and pain will be no more, for the first things have passed away' (Revelation 21:4), just as the laws of nature of this world are perfectly adapted to the character of its freely

3. See J. C. Polkinghorne, *Faith, Science and Understanding*, SPCK/Yale University Press, 2000, ch 5.3.

evolving process, through which the old creation has made itself.

The equally necessary continuity between the old and new creations lies in the fact that the latter is the redeemed transform of the former. The pattern for this is the resurrection of Christ where, as we have already emphasised, the Lord's risen body is the eschatological transform of his dead body. This implies that the new creation does not arise from a radically novel creative act *ex nihilo*, but as a redemptive act *ex vetere*, out of the old.[4]

Important theological consequences flow from this understanding. The pressing question of why the Creator brought into being this vale of tears if it is the case that God can eventually create a world that is free from suffering, here finds its answer. God's total creative intent is seen to be intrinsically a two-step process: first the old creation, allowed to explore and realise its potentiality at some metaphysical distance from its Creator; then the redeemed new creation which, through the Cosmic Christ, is brought into a freely embraced and intimate relationship with the life of God.

A further consequence of this understanding is that it clearly establishes the value of the old creation, since it affords the raw material for eschatological transformation into the new creation. An other-worldly negation of a duty of environmental care for this present world is thereby made impossible. I find this to be a firmer and more realistic basis for the affirmation of the worth of the present world than that which might be provided by dubious utopian or millenarian speculations.

4. J. C. Polkinghorne, *Science and Christian Belief/The Faith of a Physicist*, SPCK/Princeton University Press, 1994, p. 167.

It is, of course, the transmuted 'matter' of the new creation that will be the setting for human re-embodiment in the resurrection life. Paul was emphatic that 'flesh and blood cannot inherit the kingdom of God, nor does the perishable inherit the imperishable' (1 Corinthians 15:50). Much of the fifteenth chapter of 1 Corinthians is devoted to Paul's wrestling with what this discontinuity within continuity might mean, making use of the science of his day (notably the image of the seed that 'dies'; 1 Corinthians 15:35–41). We might try the same endeavour with the aid of contemporary scientific resources, but I think that we will fare no better in terms of any attempted detailed discussion of the nature of the new creation. One thing, however, we may reasonably anticipate.

In this universe, space, time and matter are all mutually interlinked in the single package deal of general relativity. It seems reasonable to suppose that this linkage is a general feature of the Creator's will. If so, the new creation will also have its 'space' and 'time' and 'matter'. The most significant theological consequence of this belief is the expectation that there will be 'time' in the world to come.

The new creation will not be a timeless world of 'eternity', but a temporal world whose character is everlasting. (It will contain music, that specifically temporal form of art.) Just as it is intrinsic to humanity that we should be embodied, so it is intrinsic to humanity that we are temporal beings. One must recognise, however, that this conclusion runs counter to a good deal of eschatological thinking. Wolfhart Pannenberg, for example, takes a strongly pessimistic view of the value of time, believing that 'temporality is of a piece with

the structural sinfulness of our life'.[5] Therefore, for him, fulfilment is impossible 'without an end of time'.[6] In an earlier
writing, he had stated that 'the truth of time lies beyond the
self-centredness of our experience of time as past, present
and future. The truth of time is the concurrence of all events
in an eternal present'.[7] Behind this seems to lie a neopla-
tonic conviction that the timeless is superior to the temporal.
For Pannenberg the meaning of life is in its totality, albeit a
totality purged from the dissonance of sin. On this view, the
attainment of full meaning requires a full end. In this book, I
adopt an altogether more dynamic picture.

Moltmann also takes a highly qualified view of the value,
and hence the ultimate significance, of temporality.[8] For him,
the concept of the fulness of times leads to the idea that eschatologically there will be the bringing of the whole of present
history into a single focus:

> In the 'restoration of all things', all times will return and—
> transformed and transfigured—will be taken up into the
> aeon of the new creation. In the eternal creation all the
> times that in God's creative resolve were fanned out will
> also be gathered together. The unfurled times of history
> will be rolled up as a scroll, as Revelation 5 intimates.[9]

(The last remark is a curious piece of exegesis.) This coming
together of all ages will be accommodated within what Moltmann calls 'aeonic time'. This he understands to be cyclical
in nature. 'Irreversible historical time is replaced by reversible
time, as a reflection of God's eternity. . . . The preferred

5. W. Pannenberg, *Systematic Theology 3*, Eerdmans, 1998, p. 561.
6. Ibid., p. 587.
7. Quoted in J. Hick, *Death and Eternal Life*, Collins, 1976, p. 222.
8. J. Moltmann, *The Coming of God*, SCM Press, 1996, pp. 279–95.
9. Ibid., pp. 294–95.

images for eternal life are therefore dance and music, as ways of describing what is hardly imaginable in this impaired life'.[10] Even if the circle were to be replaced by the more progressive symbol of the spiral, there is a certain repetitive dullness in the image offered to us here, with its implied resistance to the concept of creative change. A more dynamic notion of perfection is surely required, even to the possibility of admitting that not everything that has been will be preserved in being. Richard Bauckham is right to say that 'in assessing Moltmann's eschatology, it needs to be considered whether transience cannot be evaluated in a more discriminating way.[11]

Luco Van den Brom is blunter in his criticism of both Pannenberg and Moltmann. Both are thinkers who lay stress on the role of the future but, nevertheless, Van den Brom believes that 'in spite of all the historical dynamics suggested by its use of future tense conceptuality', their picture leads to the rejection of an ultimate role for temporality, in a way that implies the negation of process. He considers the idea 'more deterministic than any traditional doctrine of decrees [as in Calvinism] has ever been. Its deterministic eschatology neglects the value of history that is supposed to be saved in the first place'.[12] Indeed, elsewhere Moltmann himself sees the need for the fulness of times to include the continuation and progressive fulfilment of process, when he acknowledges that the incompleteness of our present lives 'makes us think of an ongoing history after death with our lives as we have lived them'.[13]

10. Ibid., p. 295.

11. R. Bauckham, *God Will Be All in All*, T & T Clark, 1999, p. 12

12. L. Van den Brom, 'Eschatology and Time', in D. Fergusson and M. Sarot (eds.), *The Future as God's Gift*, T & T Clark, 2000, p. 165.

13. Moltmann, *Coming of God*, p. 116.

I strongly disagree with any implication that the value of human temporal experience is ultimately a misapprehension or a deficiency. In my view, part of the continuity that we may expect to hold between the two halves of God's great creative/redemptive act is that the patient God who acts through temporally unfolding process in the old creation, will continue to act in a similar fashion in the unfolding fulfilment of the new creation. In chapter 11 we shall explore what this might mean for the nature of human eschatological destiny. We need to rid ourselves of the vestiges of the platonic notion that perfection is static, and to replace it with an altogether more dynamic concept. Music should indeed be our guiding image, not sculpture. Each one of Bach's thirty Goldberg variations is perfect in itself and we do not need to opt for just one of them. They present us with an image of change without either repetition or loss. It is the exploration of the endless variations of divine perfection that will constitute the harmony of the heavenly realm. How otherwise could finite beings encounter the Infinite? Not that even such an exploration will begin to exhaust the unlimited riches of the divine nature. A simple example from mathematics can make the latter point. A mind capable of adding one unit at a time could successively explore the infinity of the integers, but the greater infinity of the real numbers would still remain unknown, for such a mind would have no access to the numerical wealth that lies between zero and one.

Speaking of the new as arising from the transformation of the old might seem to encourage a simple notion of their successive relationship, so that future 'time' is the continuation of present time beyond its natural end. Yet the occurrence of the resurrection of Christ as an event within, as well as beyond, present history, suggests the necessity for a more nuanced notion of the connection between old and new. It is possible, and theologically desirable, to consider a subtler relationship rather than simple succession. Mathematicians can readily think of the spacetime of the old creation and the 'spacetime' of the new creation as being in different dimensions of the totality of divinely sustained reality, with resurrection involving an information-bearing mapping between the two, and the redemption of matter as involving a projection from the old onto the new. Such a picture offers some partial insight into the nature of the appearances of the risen Christ, as arising from limited intersections between these two worlds. It also offers a possible response to the observation that, if the new creation simply follows on from the old, God will have to wait an awful long time if our universe is, in fact going to expand for ever, so that its expected future will be an infinitely prolonged dying fall.[14]

If something like this is indeed the case, it offers us ways of thinking about how life in this world and life in the world to come might be related to each other. Much traditional Christian thinking about an intermediate state between death and resurrection has been in terms of 'soul sleep', a kind of suspended animation awaiting the restoration of full humanity. Our idea of the information-bearing patterns of souls being held in the mind of God has some obvious kinship with this picture. Some modern theologians, including Karl Rahner, have thought about the matter differently, supposing that,

14. Other possible responses would include either God's bringing the dying fall to an end once it had gone beyond a certain level of diminished cosmic activity at which creativity had effectively ceased, or to query whether divine experience of created temporality is measured on human scientific scales (see Psalm 90:4).

though we all die at different times in this world, we may all arrive simultaneously on the day of resurrection in the world to come. If time and 'time' are related in the way we have been discussing, this would clearly be a coherent possibility, with mappings from different times all leading to the same 'time' in the world to come. This would constitute the modern version of what we might suppose Paul to have been expressing when he spoke of us all being changed 'in the twinkling of an eye' as the perishable puts on imperishability (1 Corinthians 15:52–53). It might also help us with the understanding of the meaning of a verse, much discussed by writers on eschatology, in which Jesus says to the penitent thief, 'Truly I tell you, today you will be with me in Paradise' (Luke 23:43).

ALL CREATION

One further topic remains to be discussed in relation to the new creation. What are we to expect will be the destiny of non-human creatures? They must have their share in cosmic hope, but we scarcely need suppose that every dinosaur that ever lived, let alone all of the vast multitude of bacteria that have constituted so large a fraction of biomass throughout the history of terrestrial life, will each have its own individual eschatological future. On the other hand, the kind of theological thinking that has too exclusively an anthropocentric focus surely takes too narrow a view of God's creative purposes. It is conceivable that this eschatological dilemma can be resolved by according significance in non-human creatures more to the type than to the token. Many people who are respectful of animals would nevertheless consider it permissible to cull individuals in order to preserve the herd. Perhaps there will be lions in the world to come but not every lion that has ever lived. If that is the case, lionhood will have also to share in the dialectic of eschatological continuity and discontinuity, in accordance with the prophet vision that in 'the new heavens and the new earth . . . the wolf and the lamb shall feed together, the lion shall eat straw like the ox' (Isaiah 65:17 and 25). Particularly interesting, in a speculative way, is the question of the destiny of pets, who could be thought to have acquired enhanced individual status through their interactions with humans. Perhaps they will have a particular role to play in the restored relationships of the world to come.

Some kind of balance between transience and preservation is certainly necessary. In his integrative eschatology,[15] Moltmann rightly insists that individual destinies and universal destinies are opposite sides of the same eschatological coin. Yet, when he writes that 'resurrection has become the universal "law" of creation, not merely for human beings, but for animals, plants, stones and all cosmic systems as well',[16] the eschaton is in danger of becoming a museum collection of all that has ever been. It is hard to believe that individual stones as such either have or need an ultimate destiny.

15. Moltmann, *Coming of God*, pp. xiv–xvi.
16. J. Moltmann, *The Way of Jesus Christ*, SCM Press, 1990, p. 258.

CHAPTER ELEVEN

The Four Last Things

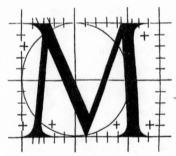UCH traditional Christian eschatological thinking has centred on the Four Last Things: Death; Judgement; Heaven; Hell. An emphasis, particularly strong in the early twentieth century, on the all-pervasive role of eschatology in relation to theology has had the curious and unfortunate side effect of tending to dissolve concern with truly ultimate matters. The more 'realised' one's view, the less there seemed to wait for. Those of us who adopt the more balanced stance of an inaugurated eschatology will not be content with a neglect of the Four Last Things. Niels Gregersen has recently written in defence of a revival of concern with final questions, commenting

> In my view, a leading motif in the conception of the Last Judgement is that there will *at some point* (not now!) be an unambiguous revelation of what *already now* is the case

(but concealed!). . . . The futurity of eschatological imagery manifests that judgement is not of our determining.[1]

I believe that the Four Last Things provide a convenient framework within which to continue our theological reflections on the life of the world to come.

DEATH

Although the New Testament quite often uses the peaceful metaphor of falling asleep to represent the death of believers (Acts 7:60; 1 Corinthians 15: 6 and 18; 1 Thessalonians 4:13 and 15; 2 Peter 3:4), Christian thinking has always faced unflinchingly the reality of death. The deeply moving episode of Gethsemane shows that, though Jesus accepted the cup that it was his Father's will that he should drink, he shared the human condition to the full, even to the extent of experiencing a natural reluctance in the face of mortality. A resolute acceptance can make death into the final act in this world that expresses a commitment to trust in the faithfulness of God. This thought is beautifully expressed in lines from a Charles Wesley hymn:

> Still let me prove thy perfect will,
> my acts of faith and love repeat;
> till death thine endless mercies seal,
> and make the sacrifice complete.

For the Christian, the darkness of death is accepted in the light of the the hope of resurrection thereafter.

There has been a strong Christian tradition, particularly indebted to Augustine in its development, that sees human

1. N. Gregersen, 'The Final Crucible', in D. Fergusson and M. Sarot (eds.), *The Future as God's Gift*, T & T Clark, 2000, p. 172.

death as the consequence of human sin. Paul expressed the idea when he wrote to the Romans concerning Adam that 'just as sin came into the world through one man and death came through sin, so death spread to all because all have sinned' (Romans 5:12). With our evolutionary understanding of the history of terrestrial life and of hominid origins, we can no longer hold this view literally in relation to the fact of physical death. However, in mythic mode the discourse conveys a truth about humankind whose coming to be must have had some counterpart in the history of our ancestors. As self-consciousness dawned—itself a process as difficult to envisage as it is certain that it happened—there would surely also have dawned a form of God-consciousness. The episode that theologians call the Fall can then be understood as a turning away from God into the human self, by which our ancestors became curved in upon themselves and alienated from the divine reality. This was not the cause of physical death but it gave to that experience the spiritual dimension of mortality. Self-conscious beings could anticipate their future death, but at the same time they had become divorced from the God who is the only ground for hope of a destiny beyond that death. Thus humanity became prey to that sadness and frustration at the thought of human transience that we may call mortality. In that sense 'death'—the bitterness of mortality—had truly come into the world and passed to all.[2] I think this interpretation does the theological work that Paul wants it to do in Romans 5.

Some Christian traditions have seen death as drawing a bottom line under a human life and thereby establishing

2. J. C. Polkinghorne, *Science and Theology*, SPCK/Fortress, 1998, pp 63–65.

its status with respect to eschatological destiny in the life to come. Hence the concern with a good death and the dread of sudden death, which might come upon a person unprepared. For centuries, a staple of Christian spirituality was the production of a wealth of little treatises on *Ars Moriendi* (the art of dying). To die in a state of grace, shriven of the sins of this world, was the great completion to achieve in life, even if it were attained at the very last moment 'between the stirrup and the ground'.

How differently the contemporary mind views the matter. Sudden death, that serves to eliminate the anxieties of dying, is what many people today would most wish for as the ending of their lives. This attitude is an aspect of the modern taboo on mortality, the desire to hide away death, locating it preferably in some sanitised and isolated hospital setting, as if it did not really exist.

This strategy of trying to avert attention from the one great human certainty is foolish and ineffective. Yet there is reason to protest theologically at those earlier notions that saw death as irrevocably fixing a person's eternal destiny. Just as the appeal to continuity based on divine consistency has led us to expect that the life of the world to come will be characterised by God's working through unfolding redemptive process rather than through instantaneous magic, so we may also project into that world the love and mercy that God displays to us in this life. One cannot suppose that an iron curtain comes down at death and God says to those caught on the wrong side of it, 'You had your chance for seventy or eighty years and now it's too late. No more mercy or forgiveness!' Surely the God of everlasting love is always ready, like the father in Jesus' parable, to meet the returning prodigal whenever he comes to himself and returns to his true home. To say this is by no means to imply that the decisions we make in this life are trivial or irrelevant. Those who knowingly turn from God in this world will find it correspondingly more painful and more difficult to make that turn of repentance if it is delayed to the life to come. Yet it is surely also true, in the mercy of God, that those who, through circumstances beyond their control, have never truly heard the gospel of Christ, or never had a real opportunity to respond to its call in this life, will not be denied that opportunity in the clearer light of the divine presence in the world of the new creation.

JUDGEMENT

The foregoing considerations lead us naturally to engage with the question of the nature of the judgement to come. There are many stern images and warnings of this judgement to be found in the pages of the New Testament (Matthew 10:28; 13:37–43; 25:31–46; Romans 2:6–10; 2 Thessalonians 1:5–10; Hebrews 9:27; Revelation 20:11–15; and so on). Some of these are associated with the depiction of cruel sufferings imposed upon unrepentant sinners. Such images have inspired generations of hell-fire preachers to seek to reduce their hearers to an abject fear as part of what they presumed to regard as preparation for the gospel. The doom carving on the tympanum over the west door, or a painting of the Last Judgement on the walls, are common features of well-preserved medieval churches. What are we to make of this use of terror in the service of the God of love?

A number of things must be said. One is that God is a holy God whose kingdom is the realm of moral purity. 'Nothing unclean will enter [the holy city], nor anyone who practices abomination or falsehood' (Revelation 21:27). We have already discussed in human terms the costliness of true forgiveness (p. 97). The cross of Christ is the measure of the costliness of divine forgiveness. Sin is no trivial matter, but it is in fact a deadly matter (Romans 6:23), a spiritual gangrene that must be dealt with by excision. Judgement is the acknowledgement of moral seriousness. One reason for much of the violence of scriptural imagery in this respect is that it serves to underline the fact that judgement is no superficial matter nor one of mere conventionality but the recognition of the nature of reality. A similar point is made in Dante's *Inferno*. Although this great poem contains sadistic elements, there is an underlying congruity between the sinners and the forms of their punishments that serves to emphasise the gravity of the natural consequences of unrepented sin. The lustful are tossed restlessly forever in a howling wind that blows them away, just as their self-indulgent passions did in this life; the gluttonous are sunk in a sodden mire in mutual isolation, mirroring their previous wallowings in selfish pleasure; and so on.

The second thing to say is that, as we read these passages, we tend to assign persons unambiguously to the company of the blessed or to the company of the damned. There may be another way to read them. Take that haunting parable of judgement, the sheep and the goats (Matthew 25:31–46). To the sheep the Lord says that when he was hungry they fed him, when he was thirsty they gave him drink, all this fulfilled in terms of Christ's anonymous presence in the poor and needy. To the goats, the Lord says the opposite. Their neglect of the poor was their neglect of him. These words present us with a formidable challenge, but if we take them seriously, do we find ourselves unambiguously in one company or the other? More likely, we recognise that sometimes (perhaps by no means often enough) we have met the needs of the Lord in the needs of the marginalised; sometimes (perhaps too often) we have not. We are neither wholly sheep nor wholly goat. Perhaps then, judgement is not simply a retrospective assessment of what we have been but it includes the prospective offer of what we might become. Perhaps judgement is a process rather than a verdict. Perhaps its fire is the cleansing fire that burns away the dross of our lives; its sufferings the consequence of the knife wielded by the divine Surgeon who wounds to heal. Perhaps judgement builds up the sheep and diminishes the goat in each one of us. We are approaching here a concept of purgatorial judgement, an issue to which I shall return.

In John's gospel, we are given a different image of judgement, an image that is stern and destructive of all easy human complacency, but one that could never be debased into the picture of a kind of testy rejection by an angry God.

> And this is the judgement, that light has come into the world, and people loved darkness rather than light because their deeds were evil. For all who do evil hate the light and do not come to the light, so that their deeds may not be exposed. But those who do what is true come to the light, so that it may clearly be seen that their deeds have been done in God. (John 3:19-21)

The Johannine concept of judgement is not that of a divine rejection but of a human self-exposure. In the face of reality ('the light'), we reveal by our actions who we really are. If we can accept this revelation, we are enabled to know ourselves and to recognise our needs. The positive side of this image is expressed in the first epistle of John: 'when he is revealed, we will be like him, for we shall see him as he is' (1 John 3:2). Once again there is a hint of salvific process, for we can scarcely suppose that Christ will be taken in at a glance.

Augustine, in that great eschatological work *The City of God*, had reached a similar concept of judgement as involving naked self-knowledge. His motivation was rather odd, arising from asking how the one book of life (Revelation 20:12) could be read out without intolerably protracting the proceedings. His conclusion, however, was consonant with what we have been suggesting: 'a kind of divine power will ensure that all the actions, good and bad, of every individual will be recalled to mind and presented to the mind's view with miraculous speed, so that each person's knowledge will accuse or excuse his conscience'.[3]

The concept of judgement as the painful encounter with reality, in which all masks of illusion are swept away, is powerful and convincing. It is also basically a hopeful image, for it is only in the recognition and acknowledgement of reality that there can reside the hope of salvation. It has some resonance with a different image used by Paul:

> For no one can lay any foundation other than the one that has been laid; that foundation is Jesus Christ. Now if anyone builds on the foundation with gold, silver, precious stones, wood, hay, straw—the work of each builder will become visible, for the Day will disclose it, because it will be revealed by fire, and fire will test what sort of work each has done. If what has been built on the foundation survives, the builder will receive a reward. If the work is burned, the builder will suffer loss; the builder will be saved, but only as through fire. (1 Corinthians 3:11-15)

3. St. Augustine, *The City of God*, XX, 20.

It is in the purging fire of judgement that there lies our hope of purification and redemption. Just as a plant in a darkened cave will respond to the slightest glimmer of light that draws its growth in that direction, so we may hope that the slightest positive response to the light of God's presence will be enough to initiate in us the final work of salvation. Properly conceived, judgement is the divine antidote to human sin, just as resurrection is the divine antidote to human mortality.

One further thing needs to be said about judgement. So far we have spoken about it as if it were simply a process involving individuals and God. Yet, if there is a systemic and social dimension to sinfulness, as there certainly is, Miroslav Volf is surely right to emphasise that judgement also possesses a corresponding dimension, particularly when it is understood as being part of a redemptive process. 'If sin has an inalienable social dimension, and if redemption aims at the establishment of the order of peace . . . then the divine embrace of both victim and perpetrator must be understood as leading to their mutual embrace'.[4]

HEAVEN

The emphasis that we have been developing on creaturely process and temporality, as much in the new creation as in the old, leads to the expectation that eschatological fulfilment will prove to be an everlasting unfolding of salvific encounter with God, rather than a timeless moment of beatific illumination. The life of heaven will be lived in the presence of the divine reality, but the exploration by finite creatures of the infinite

4. M. Volf, *Ends*, p. 262.

riches of that reality will be unending. We shall enter further and further into that pantheistic experience.

Already in the fourth century, Gregory of Nyssa had expressed such a developmental hope:

> Thus though the new grace we may obtain is greater than we had before, it does not put a limit on our final goal; rather, for those who are rising to perfection, the limit of the good that is attained becomes the beginning of the discovery of higher goods. Thus they never stop rising, moving from one new beginning to the next, and the beginning of ever greater graces is never limited of itself. For the desire of those who thus rise never rests in what they already understand; but by an ever greater and greater desire, the soul keeps rising constantly to another which lies ahead, and thus it makes its way through ever higher regions towards the Transcendent.[5]

The first stages of this eschatological journey will surely involve that encounter with the holy reality of God that we have called judgement, together with the associated cleansing from those many unrealities with which our lives have been laden. This purgative process will be an indispensable preparation for the more profound engagements with the life of the holy God that lie beyond it. If this is right, some revalued and re-expressed concept of purgatory seems to be an essential component in eschatological thinking. Of course the account must be demythologised to free it from those transactional crudities of late medieval thinking that played their part in leading to the Reformation. We cannot buy time off through Indulgences.

Dante gives us a wonderful picture of the hopefulness of

5. Quoted in J. Hick, *Death and Eternal Life*, Collins, 1976, p. 422.

purgatory in his *Divine Comedy*. As men and women move up the mountain that links earth to heaven, the whole scene re-echoes with alleluias as each soul takes a further heavenward step. However, even Dante's imagination faltered somewhat in describing the joys of heaven itself, at whose centre is the river of light and the heavenly rose, where

> High phantasy lost power and here broke off;
> Yet as a wheel moves smoothly, free from jars,
> My will and my desire were turned by love,
>
> The love that moves the sun and the other stars.[6]

In the penultimate line, we may perceive a hint of the answer to a problem that has perplexed some who have thought about the life of heaven. If the company of the blessed is the company of the truly free, as we must surely suppose it to be, how can heaven be proof against a second Fall, the rebellious exercise of that freedom which would then destroy the heavenly harmony? I think that the answer lies along these lines: Thomas Aquinas believed that the essence of freedom is consent to the good, for who would wish for anything other than the good? The sinful distortions of this life often make people misapprehend in grievously hurtful ways where the good actually lies. In the clear light of the divine presence, shining in the new creation, such disastrous errors will no longer be possible. We shall see the good, and freely and totally consent to it. Our wills and our desires will be turned by love. That will be the free source of celestial stability. As Augustine said in the *Confessions*, we shall find our true rest in God. Volf calls it a state of 'new innocence'.[7]

6. Dante, *Paradiso*, Canto xxxiii, lines 142–45.
7. Wolf, *Ends*, p. 274.

People, including some Christian believers, sometimes say that they do not wish for everlasting life. More years than this world provides, maybe, but not unending days. Even the man who said that when he went to heaven he would play golf everyday, might sicken of the game after a few thousand years. Even less attractive is the caricature notion of sitting on a cloud, eternally strumming a harp. Of course, these trivial images are totally inadequate. What awaits us is the unending exploration of the inexaustible riches of God, a pilgrim journey into deepest reality that will always be thrilling and life-enhancing. 'What no eye has seen, nor ear heard, nor human heart conceived, what God has prepared for those who love him' (1 Corinthians 2:9; derived from Isaiah 64:4). Volf reminds us that Gregory of Nyssa argued persuasively that 'on account of the infinity of God . . . the state of perfection is one of unlimited progress'.[8] Volf sees heaven as a state of pure joy, in which all the discords, enmities and injuries of the old creation find their harmonious reconciliation and healing. He says that 'we should think of the time of the world to come not as "fulness of time", but as "reconciliation of times". The difference lies precisely in the refusal of closure, which the term "fulness" suggests'.[9]

This picture of unending fulfilment within the world of the new creation is, for me, a much more convincing image of the life post mortem than that which John Hick has proposed.[10] He suggests that we shall live many lives in a succession of different worlds, until we attain an egoless state in

8. Ibid., p. 276.
9. Ibid., p. 275. He is partly protesting at some of the concepts that we criticised earlier (pp. 000-000).
10. Hick, *Eternal Life*, ch. 20.

which embodiment and temporality are no longer necessary. Hick is greatly influenced by a desire to find a synthesis between the Abrahamic faiths and Eastern religions. I am unable to relinquish the Abrahamic conviction of the enduring significance of the human individual in God's sight.

Any parish priest or pastor is asked many times by bereaved persons, 'Will I see my loved one again?' Since human relationships are constitutive of our humanity, and central sources of human good, one can reply unhesitatingly, 'Yes— nothing of good will be lost in the Lord'. In fact, what can at best be only a partial good in this world will be redeemed to become a total good in the world to come. Human hope is a community hope; human destiny is a collective destiny. Fulfilment lies in our incorporation into the one body of Christ.

HELL

God's offer of mercy and forgiveness is not withdrawn at death but, rather, divine love is everlasting. Nevertheless, no one will be carried into the kingdom of heaven against their will by an overpowering act of divine power. Therefore we must ask the question of whether, in the end, the resistance of even the most stubborn and contemptuous of sinners will melt in the fire of God's love, or whether there will be those who resist God for ever? In the latter case, those who make an enduring decision against God have condemned themselves to hell. They are not there because they have been hurled there by an angry God, but because they have made their resolute choice to exclude the divine life from their lives. As the preachers say, the gates of hell are locked on the inside.

If that is the case, hell is a place of boredom rather than

a place of unending torture. Its colour is grey rather than red. For an imaginative depiction of hell we should turn not to Dante, but to C. S. Lewis's *Great Divorce*,[11] where hell is a dreary town lost down a crack in the floor of heaven. Its inhabitants are taken, from time to time, on a bus trip to the celestial realm to see if they would like to transfer there. Sadly, most of them return, unable to endure the bright reality of heaven.

If hell is the place where the divine life has been deliberately excluded, then some have thought that its inhabitants will eventually fade away into nothingness, because the divine Spirit has habitually been denied its sustaining work in their lives. There is some persuasiveness in this notion of annihilation (sometimes called the idea of conditional immortality), though it would also represent the final creaturely defeat of the divine purpose of love. It is hard to know what to think, just as it is similarly hard to know whether the universalist hope, that in the end and in every life, God's love will always be victorious, implies that though there is, so to speak, a hell, ultimately it will be found to be empty. Perhaps these uncertainties are a necessary dimension of eschatological thinking pursued within the confines of this present world. If one were certain of eventual universal salvation, it might encourage a moral indifferentism and a reliance on cheap grace. We detect such an attitude in the words of the dying poet Heine. When asked if he were concerned about the consequences of his dissolute life, he said, 'God will pardon me. That is his line of business'. On the other hand, if we were certain that there are some who will be in hell for ever, we might ask why it was that

11. C. S. Lewis, *The Great Divorce*, Geoffrey Bles, 1946.

God allowed them to be part of the divine creation at all. Not all our perplexities can be resolved in this life.

We have come to the end of our thinking about the character of the life to come. It is not unfitting that the final thoughts of this chapter should refer to issues about which we find it hard to reach definite conclusions. In many cases, the appropriate answer must be 'Wait and see'. Yet we may so wait confident in hope, because that hope is grounded in the everlasting faithfulness of God, the One who raised our Lord Jesus Christ from the dead. Without that hope, the gospel is incomplete (1 Corinthians 15:19). While there is a necessary tentativity about the details of much Christian eschatological thinking, there is also a theological indispensibility about the quest for as coherent and credible an articulation of the Ends of God as we can manage to achieve.

CHAPTER TWELVE

The Significance of the End

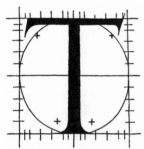HE story of Jesus would be incomplete without the resurrection. We would know about his teaching and the claims that marvellous works were done by him. We would know that he was unjustly condemned to a cruel death. But we would not be sure how we should assess all this. Was he defeated? Was he deluded? Or what exactly was he? The ambiguity inherent in the incomplete story of Jesus is resolved by God's raising him on the third day. Here is the ground for assurance that Jesus is indeed God's Lord and Christ.

There is a similar ambiguity about the story of the universe. If it simply ends with the bang of collapse or the whimper of decay, it runs into incompleteness. Is the cosmos, after all, as pointless as Steven Weinberg believes, so that its story is really a tale of chaos? Are the deep order of the world, and the fruitfulness of its history, hints of its being a creation, or are they just happy accidents in a meaningless process? Are

139

human intuitions of hope windows into a divine reality, or are they comforting illusions that offer us delusive support as we battle to survive? If the universe really is God's creation, the ambiguity of its past history and present prospects will have to be resolved in its final end. In *The Four Quartets*, T. S. Eliot struggled with how meaning is to be found in the coinherence of beginning and ending. 'In my beginning is my end'. The reason that eschatology is such an indispensable element in theological thinking is that it responds to the question of the total meaningfulness of the present creation, a meaning that can only finally be found beyond science's extrapolation of contemporary history.

COMPARISONS

Eschatology is the keystone of the edifice of theological thinking, holding the whole building together. Among the twentieth century theologians to whose work we have made reference above, there is wide agreement that this is the case. Yet as we explored eschatological themes, it became clear that there are some important differences in the way in which the discourse is framed, particularly between the concerns and concepts that are significant for mainstream systematic theologians and the concerns and concepts that are significant for a scientist-theologian like the present writer. These differences give rise to differing ways in which the common issues are approached. This contrast is a consequence of different attitudes to three aspects of the task in hand.

The first difference concerns the timescales over which thinking about the present form of creation is allowed to range. The writings of the systematic theologians seldom seem to reflect the expectation that cosmic history will continue for many billions of years and that, before its foreseeable end, humanity and all forms of carbon-based life will have vanished from the universe. Of course, it might be that divine intervention will ring down the cosmic curtain before science expects, but it seems unwise to suppose so. After all, God might have started off creation in a more developed state than that represented by the almost uniform expanding ball of energy that is our picture of the universe immediately post big bang, but we do not think that God did so. If that is the case, and God allowed primeval process to unfold over billions of years, why should we not expect the same to be true of cosmic ending. (Though see n. 14 of chapter 10 for an alternative possibility.) We should not underestimate divine patience—hence our emphasis throughout on the developing nature of creaturely being. Nor should we underestimate the scope of God's salvific intentions for future generations. Some people in the early church may have expected an imminent parousia because it seemed to them that after the climactic event of Christ's resurrection there was not much point in history's continuing further. Yet that eschatological event within history is the basis for all of what will be fulfilled beyond history, and it is not for human thought to set limits to the extent of the ultimate fruitfulness that the resurrection has inaugurated (cf. Hebrews 2:10).

Considering history seriously only on a human scale allows the systematic theologians to be in some ways less radical in their expectation of ultimate eschatological transformation than is the case for the scientist-theologians. It is not 'late in time', as the carol says, that we behold Christ come at Bethlehem, but early in time, cosmically considered. The parousia is by no means yet overdue. The threats that the future contains are not simply those of ecological pollution or nuclear devastation, serious though these issues are. It is too anthropocentric to write, as Jürgen Moltmann did, that we are living in a 'nuclear and ecological end time' and to 'deduce from this that before the final end of history there will be a concentration of humanity's both constructive and destructive opportunities'.[1] To criticise this stance is not to deny the importance of human political history but to recognise that there are even greater issues at stake. (After all, the explosion of the Sun into its red giant phase will eventually destroy the whole Earth.) It is the human scale of Moltmann's thinking that encourages him, while rejecting modern utopianism, to consider a millenarian scenario as a kind of conceivable transition between history and the eschaton: 'millenarian expectation mediates between world history and the new world there . . . christocracy . . . is the transition from the world's present condition to its coming consummation'.[2] To the scientist-theologian this all sounds a little too cosily terrestrial.

Behind Moltmann's thinking, and despite a stronger engagement in his later writing with apocalyptic ideas, there seems to lie a conception of the completion of history as part of a relatively smooth transition from the old creation to the new creation.[3] The millennium is to play the bridging role. Perhaps there is a residual reluctance here to give up some ultimate form of political hope within the course of present history, even if this is to be understood in end-time, rather than utopian, terms.

1. J. Moltmann, *The Coming of God*, SCM Press, 1996, p. 201.
2. Ibid.
3. See R. Bauckham, *God Will Be All in All*, T & T Clark, 1999, pp. 123–47.

To the scientist-theologian this manner of speaking does not appeal as a way of engaging the eschatological tension between continuity and discontinuity. I have argued that the new creation must be endowed with a totally different 'physical fabric' from that of the old creation and, of course, this must be on a universe-wide scale. This consideration implies that, though the new creation is the transform of the old creation, the distinction between the two must be as sharp as that between death and resurrection. The one cannot be parlayed into the other.

Moltmann and Pannenberg express their recognition of the need for critical change when they portray eschatological discontinuity in terms of the transformation of temporality. Moltmann appeals to the elusive concept of aeonic time, while Pannenberg speaks of the end of time altogether. In contrasting ways, both of them believe that the temporal totality of present history is to find its fulfilment in being focussed into a unity. It is not entirely clear what this could mean but, from the point of view of this book, the resulting negation of the role of continuing process within the eschaton is a profoundly unsatisfactory form of discontinuity.

Thus the second point of difference is one that we have already considered in some detail (pp. 132–136). It concerns the value and necessity for finite embodied beings to participate in unfolding temporal process, as much in the new creation as in the old. Dynamic becoming is the form of perfection appropriate to creatures of our kind. For this reason, and in contrast to many systematic colleagues, a scientist-theologian finds it congenial and necessary to present an understanding of the kind of everlastingly exploratory character of the life of the world to come, as was attempted in chapter 11.

The final difference relates to the method by which one seeks to explore the fundamental eschatological theme of continuity/discontinuity. This is a problem that all theologians have to grapple with and no one can proceed without some measure of conjecture. A significant contrast between systematic theologians and scientist-theologians lies in the manner in which the latter feel the need to test proposed concepts against motivated suppositions, the latter being derived from present experience but extrapolated beyond it, in a way that the discussion of chapters 9 and 10 illustrates. However jejune such attempts must inevitably be in advance of any experience of redeemed reality, they give a modest degree of substance to eschatological thinking, in a way that seems necessary to explicate the hope to which it refers.

This strategy is an aspect of what I have called a 'bottom-up' approach to theology,[4] so natural to those whose primary intellectual formation has been in the sciences. This same stance has also been reflected in the way in which, during the past ten years or so, the science and theology community has not felt comfortable in discussing providence and divine action without some recourse to motivated conjecture about the form of the causal joint by which God might be supposed to act in the world.[5] Systematic theologians, on the other hand, seem happy to operate in a more 'top-down' manner of assertion. If the scientist theologians may sometimes appear a little pedestrian in the conjectures that they make, the systematic theologians sometimes seem a little rhetorical in the claims

---

4. J. C. Polkinghorne, *Science and Christian Belief/The Faith of a Physicist*, SPCK/Princeton University Press, 1994, pp. 4–5 and passim.

5. For a summary see J. C. Polkinghorne, *Scientists as Theologians*, SPCK, 1996, ch. 3.

that they make. One feels one has to ask the systematicians to exhibit more clearly the motivations for some of the statements that they utter. I believe that, in relation to eschatology, explorations of a bottom-up kind can help to make accessible to contemporaries those insights of a destiny beyond death, that otherwise might seem to them to be no more than implausible airy fantasies.

ESCHATOLOGICAL VERIFICATION

The experience to which eschatological hope points can play a novel and distinct role in relation to the ascertainment of theological truth. John Hick, in an early writing, pointed out that life post mortem offers the possibility of a degree of verification of Christian theistic belief that is not attainable within the limits of this present world.[6] Hick's concept of eschatological verification can be expressed in terms of his parable of the two travellers. These two men are on a journey together and as they pass through the countryside their experiences are very similar. Weariness and refreshment come to both alike. Yet one traveller believes that he is on his way to the Celestial City, while the other has no such expectation and sees the journey as an expedition without the prospect of a final fulfilment. 'During the course of their journey, the issue between them is not an experimental one'.[7] However, they interpret their experiences very differently. One sees the pleasures that travel brings as foretastes of the greater joy awaiting him, and its pains as being worth enduring for the sake of

6. J. Hick, *Faith and Knowledge* (second edition), Cornell University Press, 1966, ch. 8.

7. Ibid., p. 177.

that final happiness. The other takes the good and the bad as they come, making the best of a journey that ultimately has no point. The differences are great, but when they round the last bend, one will be proved right and the other wrong. Either the Celestial City will come into view, or the land will stretch out before them without any significant feature. The journey will prove either to have been 'Pilgrim's Progress' or 'Just one damn thing after another'. In a similar way, the eschaton will either verify or falsify Christian belief—though if the latter is the case, there will be no human person there to witness the disproof.

Hick emphasises that 'survival after bodily death would not [in itself] in the least constitute a final verification of theistic faith'.[8] It might simply indicate that nature was much richer and stranger than we had previously thought. Here, I think, his cool philosophical method rather leads him astray. Without denying the strict logic of the point being made, it seems to me, as I have said several times in the course of the foregoing pages, that the everlasting faithfulness of God seems far and away the most rationally credible basis for the possibility of a human life post mortem, and so experience of such a life would seem, in itself, at least strongly suggestive of the existence of a benevolent deity.

Nevertheless, Hick is surely right to say that the kind and quality of that life after death would be a vital element in the verification of Christian theism. It would be necessary that we should find ourselves in 'a *situation* that points unambiguously to the existence of a loving God'.[9] Certainly, finding that we

8. Ibid., p. 186.
9. Ibid., p. 187.

were caught up in the endless cycles of a world of eternal return would raise serious questions about the character of the God who had given us that kind of post mortem destiny.

Hick goes on to formulate two criteria that would have to be satisfied by the life to come if it were to constitute the eschatological verification of theism. He was writing at a time before he had entered into his present pan-religious phase, and so the first condition is that we should be given 'an experience of the fulfillment of God's purposes in ourselves, as this has been disclosed in the Christian revelation'.[10] The second condition, closely related to the first, is 'an experience of God as he has revealed himself in the person of Christ'.[11] Those of us who still hold the conviction of the uniqueness of Jesus Christ as God's self-revelation in human terms, will wish, without disrespect to our brothers and sisters in other faiths, to retain these criteria for ultimate significance formulated in these Christological terms.

Hick's first criterion is, as he observes, closely related to the concept of eternal life expressed in the gospel of John. The second criterion has a special importance for Hick as providing a test by which it could be verified that the post mortem experiences concerned really were *of God*. As a philosopher, he is worried by the fact that finite beings can never verify infinite divine characteristics, such as omnipotence or omniscience. Great but finite power, and great but finite knowledge, would already be enough to overwhelm us. (This point is related to David Hume's criticism of natural theology pursued in this present life, that it could never reveal for certain the existence

10. Ibid.
11. Ibid.

of an infinite Being.) Yet employing the Christological criterion would enable us to verify encounter with the God and Father of our Lord Jesus Christ. Hick quotes Karl Barth as saying that 'Jesus Christ is the knowability of God'.[12]

Of course, eschatological verification does not provide us here and now with a method of settling disputes about the truth of theism. But it does indicate that there is a meaningful truth claim at issue which ultimately can, and will, be settled. The traveller who arrives at the Celestial City will have made his point. We see again why eschatological thinking has such a vital role in relation to Christian theology generally. The two stand in a mutual relationship of interaction and support. As I have suggested many times in the course of my argument, belief in the faithfulness of God is the ground of eschatological hope. Equally, eschatological experience will provide the ultimate vindication of belief in that God.

ESCHATOLOGICAL CRITERIA

We may summarise a viable approach to eschatological expectation in terms of four propositions:

(1) If the universe is a creation, it must make sense everlastingly, and so ultimately it must be redeemed from transience and decay.

(2) If human beings are creatures loved by their Creator, they must have a destiny beyond their deaths. Every generation must participate equally in that destiny, in which it will receive the healing of its hurts and the restoration of its integrity, thereby participating for itself in the ultimate fulfilment of the divine purpose.

12. Ibid., p. 190.

(3) In so far as present human imagination can articulate eschatological expectation, it has to do so within the tension between continuity and discontinuity. There must be sufficient continuity to ensure that individuals truly share in the life to come as their resurrected selves and not as new beings simply given the old names. There must be sufficient discontinuity to ensure that the life to come is free from the suffering and mortality of the old creation.

(4) The only ground for such a hope lies in the steadfast love and faithfulness of God that is testified to by the resurrection of Jesus Christ.

Christian belief must not lose its nerve about eschatological hope. A credible theology depends upon it and, in turn, a Trinitarian and incarnational theology can assure us of its credibility.

Index